Wedding Toasts I'll Never Give

Center Point
Large Print

**This Large Print Book carries the
Seal of Approval of N.A.V.H.**

Wedding Toasts I'll Never Give

ADA CALHOUN

CENTER POINT LARGE PRINT
THORNDIKE, MAINE

This Center Point Large Print edition
is published in the year 2017 by arrangement with
W. W. Norton & Company, Inc.

A version of Toast 1 ran in the Modern Love column of
The New York Times as "The Wedding Toast I'll Never
Give," on July 16, 2015; Lines in Toasts 2 and 6
appeared in the Modern Love column of *The New York
Times* as "You May Call It Cheating, but We Don't,"
on September 14, 2012. Part of Toast 4 appeared in the
Lives column of *The New York Times Magazine*
as "Misery Games," on October 21, 2012.

The text of this Large Print edition is unabridged.
In other aspects, this book may vary
from the original edition.
Printed in the United States of America
on permanent paper.
Set in 16-point Times New Roman type.

ISBN: 978-1-68324-436-3

Library of Congress Cataloging-in-Publication Data

The Library of Congress has cataloged this record
under LCCN: 2017013437.

For Neal, of course

Contents

Wedding Toasts I'll Never Give

Marriage is a relationship far more engrossing than we want it to be. It always turns out to be more than we bargained for. It is disturbingly intense, disruptively involving, and that is exactly the way it was designed to be. It is supposed to be more, almost, than we can handle.

—Mike Mason,
The Mystery of Marriage, 1985

Introduction

"Do You Know Why You're Here?"

> Like everything which is not the involuntary result of fleeting emotion but the creation of time and will, any marriage, happy or unhappy, is infinitely more interesting and significant than any romance, however passionate.
>
> —W. H. Auden, "Marriage," 1970

I never give toasts at weddings. I prefer to sit quietly under the twinkling lights, enjoying other people's efforts. Some are perfect mini-sermons—but better, because at the end there's champagne. Some go rattling off the rails, and that's fun, too. At a wedding I attended recently, one groomsman paused in the middle of his toast and—unable to remember the rest of what he meant to say—just sat down.

At my own wedding, twelve years ago, my Texan father-in-law delivered a biblical homily, my New York father a witty speech, a midwestern aunt a eulogy for a late family member, and my best friend, who lives in D.C., a gentle roast. All lovely. Then an old friend of my husband's leapt up and surprised us with a poem he'd written about taxis. Fearing that this might devolve into an open-mike situation, I then thanked everyone and announced that it was time to eat.

Finding something new or helpful to say about marriage feels borderline impossible. "It's difficult to think about marriage," says a friend married for thirty years. "It's like trying to describe your own face." And so we offer clichéd advice like the dubious Ephesians paraphrase "Don't go to bed angry." (Personally, I have avoided many fights by going to bed angry and waking up to realize that I'd just been tired.)

Now in the second decade of my second marriage,* I can't look newlyweds in the eye and promise they'll never regret marrying. (Well, not sober. Maybe this is why weddings correlate with binge drinking.) I adore my husband and plan to be with him forever. I also want to run screaming from the house because the person I promised to love all the days of my life insists on falling asleep to *Frasier* reruns.

"The first twenty years are the hardest," an older woman once told me. At the time I thought she was joking. She was not.

And this is why I don't give wedding toasts—

---

*In my early twenties, I was married, literally on my lunch hour, to my Canadian boyfriend. We were divorced before we could legally rent a car.

because I'd probably end up saying that even good marriages sometimes involve flinging a remote control at the wall.

During a recent rough patch, my husband, Neal, and I took a road trip to Albany to visit the priest who married us, Father Paul J. Hartt. We stationed our nine-year-old son in the next room with a Lego set and sat on a couch before the man who, more than a decade earlier, had bound us together until death. We asked him to remind us, again, why that had been a good idea.

Father Hartt told us that the question *Do you know why you're here?* is vital to marriage, and is even expressed in the Christian wedding ceremony. He pointed to the Declaration of Consent from the Book of Common Prayer. That's the section early in "The Celebration and Blessing of a Marriage" that sounds like the vows but isn't. (It includes the phrase "Will you have this man to be your husband?")

"It's a historical holdover, but it's worth pondering whether there might be something to it today," said Hartt. He explained the Declaration's original purpose via a hypothetical:

> Like, Neal's dad and your dad decide one day that it'd be a really good thing if you two got married, because it would be

good for business. Never mind that Neal's mentally impaired and you're fourteen. So your dad one morning says, "Put a dress on. We're going to the fair." And next thing you know, you're in a church getting married. So this Declaration part was supposed to be asking you, "Do you know why you're here?" If you didn't, the church was supposed to provide refuge. Some burly deacon would sweep you away into the sacristy while we dealt with your fathers.

But I honestly believe that there are a lot of weddings over which I preside where I am not altogether sure the people know why they're there. They're certainly of age. They're certainly not imbeciles. But even after the couple has spent a lot of time together, I'm not sure they know. The problem today is that all the focus seems to be on *How do you get married?* No one's spending any time on *How do you stay married?* And I think that's a cultural crisis, actually.

"It's often tough to get couples grappling with any level of theological significance of what they're doing," said Father Don Waring, who performs fifteen weddings a year at Grace Church in Manhattan. "Most really don't seem to be able to articulate what's going to be different the day after versus the day before. This concept of making a lifelong commitment to each other, they sort of back into it. Their lives are already wound up together. . . . What's lost is *How is our life going to be different after we go through this?* I wonder if that loss of 'before versus after' is what leads to the dissolution of some marriages. There's not a grasping of the fact that you're doing something existential and theologically significant."

In the throes of romantic love, we often neglect to ponder the meaning of marriage beyond a vague (and mistaken) expectation that it will make us happy. "I'm afraid I think this rage for happiness rather vulgar," says one of the more sensible characters in George Bernard Shaw's play *Getting Married*.

"On one hand, I have a lot of compassion for couples early on," said Rabbi David Adelson. "How could they know? Like all of the challenging and worthwhile undertakings that we engage in in our lives, there's no way to know what it's going to be like. On the other hand, I think there are tons of unrealistic expectations. It's part of my task to introduce realistic ones: Marriage is a microcosm of life. It's natural to seek stability, stasis, guarantees. We want things to remain *okay*. But that's never the truth in any aspect of our lives."

. . .

The main problem with marriage may be that it's not better than the rest of life. Suffering occurs in marriage because we think it will be different—purer, deeper, gentler—than other relationships. We expect our partners and ourselves to be better—more patient, more faithful, more generous—than we are. We believe ourselves exceptional, first in the depth of our passion and then in the breadth of our failure. Some marriages really are exceptional failures—too cruel, toxic, or sad to continue. Emotional and physical abuse are clear-cut grounds for divorce. But even in marriages without these profound problems, torment is common.

"In pastoral counseling around marriages," said Father Hartt, "I've consistently found that people think what they're experiencing is a sign of their uniquely defective interpersonal drama. One thing about marriages is that they're amazingly similar."

———

I've always found that parties are better on rainy nights. I think it's because bad weather weeds out the ambivalent, the uncommitted. To leave the house in a storm, you must do the work of finding an umbrella or preparing yourself for a soaking. This requires faith that leaving your dry house will pay off, that you will travel through the cold, dark, unwelcoming night and end up somewhere better than where you left. People who only ever go to parties on sunny days miss the joy of reaching a cozy room during a downpour. People who don't marry miss both the pelting hardships of marriage and its warm rewards.

Whether religious or secular, a wedding ceremony casts a spell over the couple, renders them from that instant on *apart,* a bit, from the rest of the world. Marriage isn't an achievement, the culmination of a love affair, but, rather, the announcement of an intention to live in a new way.

Rabbi Lawrence A. Hoffman says the wedding ceremony ritualizes our grandest hopes for ourselves and for those we love: "The reason that people want to get married, I think, though they may not know it, is they have a sense that marriage means more than just the benefits of life they have already—like sharing an apartment and living together, being sexual partners and that sort of thing. They get to the point where they suspect there is more to life than that; they're looking for 'the more,' and that's what weddings ritualize."

The day after a wedding, even if nothing but the jewelry appears different—you're keeping your names, you already shared a home, a bed, friends—something important has changed. From then on, every day you stay, you keep that vow.

By staying married, we give something to ourselves and to others: hope. Hope that in steadfastly loving someone, we ourselves, for all our faults, will be loved; that the broken world will be made whole. To hitch your rickety wagon to the flickering star of another fallible human being— what an insane thing to do. What a burden, and what a gift.

Such are the thoughts I keep to myself, sitting in rented folding chairs, watching friends begin their married lives. To the newlyweds, I say congratulations, and I mean it sincerely. To say out loud the rest of what I'm thinking would be bad manners. And so I'll say it here instead.

TOAST I

Paying for Each Other's Mistakes

> If a man could receive the advantages of
> marriage without the duty of standing day
> and night at a woman's side in all sorts
> of wind and weather, then nobody would
> hesitate to get married.
> —Theodor Gottlieb von Hippel,
> *On Marriage*, 1774

While away at a conference in Minneapolis, I was awakened at dawn by a call from Neal in our New York apartment. Our son, Oliver, then eight, had just roused him with the suspicion that they might not make their seven-thirty a.m. flight to join me because it was now seven-forty and they were still at home.

The original plan had us all traveling to Minneapolis together. I would attend my conference. Neal, a musician, would do a show at a cool club. Oliver would get hotel pool time. A triple win. Beyoncé and Jay Z had just completed their "On the Run" tour, baby Blue Ivy in tow. Neal and I joked about how this would be our own version, only we would be playing to crowds of dozens rather than thousands, and instead of occupying five-star hotels, we would be staying three in a room at the downtown Super 8.

Then Neal was offered a good gig in New York for the same day we were set to leave—so he called to change his and Oliver's tickets. Changing them, he learned, was going to cost more than buying a new pair of one-way tickets out. So he did that instead, planning to use their original return tickets, not realizing that if you don't use the first leg, they cancel the second. That meant buying new, last-minute return tickets at a cost somewhere between "Ugh" and "Oh dear God, what have you done?"

Money has served as a perennial source of stress in our marriage. I grew up middle-class among liberal bohemians in downtown Manhattan. He grew up working-class in a conservative Pentecostal community in the Piney Woods of East Texas. We both freelance, and so our income varies widely from month to month. He feels rich now, while without a financial cushion (more years than not, we haven't had one at all), I walk around under a cloud of low-level anxiety, positive that we are one missed payment away from destitution.

My trick for not letting this poison our relation-ship as much as it could requires engaging in what I call "marriage math"—an advanced-placement calculus designed to quash resentment.

Sample Problem: The new tickets cost $776.

Well, Neal quit smoking in 2006. Minus a relapse in 2009, that's still nine years of saving $8 a day at least, or $26,280. When Oliver was a baby and I was working full-time, we ordered takeout constantly—maybe $8,320 a year for ages 0–3. Then Neal started cooking, and so we've saved most of that every year since—to the tune, over time, of probably about $30,000. He has only one pair of shoes at a time, which saves $400 a year, so over the 15 years we've been together, that equals $6,000. And $62,280 minus those tickets . . . he's still up more than $61K. I owe him a Cadillac.

But now my family had missed the first leg of the new itinerary, outstripping even my practiced algorithms. I imagined we would have to buy the tickets a third time, and felt the familiar money panic, coupled with rage that *his* errors were costing *me*. I'd been taking my hotel-room coffee to go to save a couple of dollars each morning. And for what? Delta owned us now, anyway.

On hold with the airline, Neal was entertaining himself by texting me sexy emojis.

Eggplant. Eggplant. Eggplant.

"Focus," I replied, with an emoji of an airplane.

Neal sent me an emoji of a flan.

We've been together since I was twenty-four and Neal was twenty-five. We married in our late twenties. By the timeline of our peers in New

York, I was a child bride. A decade later, we find ourselves listening to friends describe all the ways they will excel at being married.

"I will always be your best friend," they say, reading from wrinkled pieces of paper held in shaking hands. "I will never let you down." They use analogies of rivers, of bolts of lightning, of vines wrapping around trees. Drunk on their feelings, they strike elaborate, ludicrous bargains: to never tell a lie, to always think of each other first, to show their love every single day.

I clap along with everyone else; I love weddings. Still, there is so much I want to say.

I want to say that one day you and your husband will fight about missed flights, and you'll find yourself wistful for the days when you had to pay for only your own mistakes. I want to say that at various points in your marriage, may it last forever, you will look at this person and feel only rage. You will gaze at this man you once adored and think, *It sure would be nice to have this whole place to myself.*

Over the years, Neal and I have each fallen short of various marital vows, failing each other in significant ways. We have suffered from the stresses of parenthood, work, and coexisting in an apartment so compact it's been likened to a ship's cabin. We have had fights about everything from who to be friends with to how to handle our money to whether or not we believe enough in each other to how to park the car. We have shown each other kindness, generosity, and faith, but also irritation, hostility, and white-hot fury.

We have made big compromises. Perhaps the biggest is that he wanted to wait to have children but agreed to have a baby just two years after we married, and I wanted more kids but agreed to stick with one as long as he would let me amass an army of godchildren. And we make small compromises every day. For example, I tolerate his bags of stuff always spilling out from under our bed, and he puts up with me occasionally reorganizing the cabinets, so that it takes him an hour to find a screwdriver. Usually these things are merely annoying. Sometimes they resemble grounds for divorce.

In Zen Buddhism, meditation helps practitioners detach from the cycle of desire and suffering. In my brief stint as a religious studies major, I preferred Pure Land Buddhism, an alternate path to enlightenment for people who may find it especially difficult to detach from the world because pain is so often intertwined with joy.

One of my professors read us a poem by the Japanese poet Kobayashi Issa, who was born in 1763 and, thanks to a run of terrible luck, saw three children and his wife die in the span of just a few years. He wrote, "The world of dew is / A world of dew / And yet, and yet."

"Dew is a Buddhist symbol of impermanence," my professor said. "Issa is saying that one who understands Buddhist philosophy does not necessarily transcend pain and anguish. 'And yet, and yet' means 'I can't help crying.'"

I think about that all the time: "And yet."

Such hedging, to me, is good religion, and also the key to a successful marriage. In the course of being together forever, you come across many doubt-stoking "and yets," only some of them involving domestic air travel.

I love this person, and yet when I'm sick, he's not nurturing. And yet we don't want the same number of children. And yet I sometimes wonder what it would be like to be single again.

The longer you are with someone, the more "and yets" rack up. You love this person. Of course you plan to be together forever. And yet forever can begin to seem like a long time. Breaking up and starting fresh—which seemingly half your peers will do by the time your children reach elementary school—can begin to look like a wonderful and altogether logical proposition.

But "and yet" works the other way, too. Even during the darkest moments of my own marriage, I have felt these nagging exceptions. And yet we have this child together. And yet we still make each other laugh. And yet I still love him.

And so you don't break up, and you outlast some more of your friends' marriages.

My own parents have been married since 1974, weathering a how-much-time-do-you-have list of crises. I went to my mother for advice once when Neal and I were fighting. "How do you stay married?" I asked her. Her reply: "You don't get divorced."

At the time, I thought her response flip, but now I consider it wise. Couples who have been married forty and fifty years tell me they've been on the verge of leaving many times. And then they just . . . didn't.

Gwyneth Paltrow said, not long before her own split from Chris Martin, that her parents revealed the secret of their long marriage as: "We never wanted to get divorced at the same time."

"My parents were too poor to get divorced," my friend Rachel told me. "And so they stayed married and then it seemed too late to get divorced, and now they're glad."

Later that morning, while waiting to hear from Neal about the flights, I decided to kill time looking at nearby houses on a house-hunting app. When I used to travel alone as a teenager, I would stare at houses wherever I was and imagine what it would be like to live there. I still do that, but now I can also look on my phone and see how much they cost.

Comparing houses in Minneapolis, I found I actually preferred the cheaper, more ramshackle, family-friendly ones, like a two-bedroom that had "classic old world charm." Hardwood floors! A built-in buffet! So much better, really, than the pricier one-bedroom I would live in as a single person on the other side of Powderhorn Park, with its new ceiling fans, three cedar closets, and breakfast nook.

What would I even do with three cedar closets?

Meanwhile, still no word from Neal about the flights.

One thing I love about marriage (and I love a lot of things about marriage) is that you can have a bad day or even a bad few years, full of doubt and confusion and storming out of the house. But as long as you don't get divorced, you are no less married than couples who have it all figured out.

You can be bad at a religion and still be 100 percent that religion. Just because you take the Lord's name in vain doesn't make you suddenly a non-Christian. In fact, I think it's good theology that no matter how hard you try, you are sure to be a sinner, just as you are sure to be lousy, at least sometimes, at being married. There is perfection only in death.

Years ago at a bridal shower, a bridesmaid turned to the assembled women when the bride-to-be was in the bathroom and said of the engaged couple, "I give them five years." It was so cruel

I gasped. (That the rest of us had been thinking something similar was beside the point.) And yet that couple is still together, even as couples with far better forecasts have imploded. You just never know.

It is easy for people who have never tried to do anything as strange and difficult as being married to say marriage doesn't matter, or to condemn those who fail at it, or to mock those who even try. But there is so much beauty in the trying, and in the failing, and in the trying again. Peter renounced Jesus three times before the cock crowed. And yet he was the rock upon whom Christ built his church.

This, it turns out, is how a marriage lasts: we stay in it long enough to see things change, for good and for ill and for good again. Definitive studies or scurrilous gossip about "happy marriages" or "unhappy marriages" have nothing new to tell us. As married people, we dwell on a spectrum between happy and unhappy, in love and out of love, and we move back and forth on that line decade by decade, year by year, week by week, even hour by hour.

Hero and villain, winner and loser—in a marriage, none of these are permanent roles; the parts are recast with every new play. Within a year of our Minneapolis trip, I would miss a connecting flight through Texas, costing me—

us—$327 and my sense of superiority. Neal would respond to news of my error as if his team had just won a play-off game.

That he and I sometimes want to kill each other doesn't make ours an unhappy union. That we sometimes let each other down does not make it a failure. There is wisdom in an old Jack Benny joke: "Mary and I have been married forty-seven years, and not once have we ever had an argument serious enough to mention the word 'divorce' . . . 'murder,' yes, but 'divorce,' never." So, too, in the John Updike line "All blessings are mixed."

At weddings, I do not contradict my beaming newlywed friends when they talk about how they will gracefully succeed where nearly everyone in human history has floundered. I only wish I could tell them that in this marriage, occasionally they will suffer—and that not only will they likely endure sitcom-grade squabbles, but possibly even dark-night-of-the-soul despair.

That doesn't mean they are condemned to divorce, just that it's unlikely that they will be each other's best friend every single minute forever. And that while it's good to aim high, it's quite probable they will let each other down many times, in ways both petty and profound, that in this blissful moment they can't even fathom.

I would never say any of this out loud, of course.

But if I did, I would go on to say (assuming I had not yet been thrown out of the banquet hall): Failure is part of being human, and it is definitely part of being married. It's part of what being alive means, occasionally screwing up in expensive ways. And that's part of what marriage means: sometimes hating this other person but staying together because you promised you would. And then, days or weeks later, waking up and loving him again, loving him still.

Finally, nearly two hours after Neal's original flight left, I texted him to ask if he was still on hold with the airline.

"We just got in a cab," he replied. "Flying Air Wisconsin, baby!"

"Did you have to pay for the tickets again?" I texted.

The phone was silent. In that quiet moment, sitting in my Minneapolis hotel room, I found myself daydreaming about the one-bedroom apartment looking out onto Powderhorn Park. After waking up alone, I would brew some coffee, switch on one of my many ceiling fans, grab a robe from my largest cedar closet, and head for my breakfast nook.

"Nope," he wrote back.

And suddenly I was back in the bigger place on the cheaper side of the park. My family was coming to join me. And I was glad.

TOAST 2

The Boring Parts

Each of us must live with a full measure of loneliness that is inescapable, and we must not destroy ourselves with our passion to escape this aloneness.
—Jim Harrison, *Dalva*, 1988

An author I know says he doesn't write novels because he can't bring himself to generate "the boring parts"—the pages of plot development required to move the story along. I found myself thinking about that recently as I sat, bored, beside an outdoor motel pool teeming with June bugs, watching my son swim for the better part of an afternoon.

When our son asks to swim, Neal often remembers something urgent he has to attend to, leaving me alone in a sagging plastic lawn chair, periodically rummaging in my purse for things Oliver can retrieve from the bottom of the pool: bobby pins, a ring, a Matchbox car, change. Any attempt to remove him from the water before at least two hours have elapsed is treated as a violation of the Geneva Conventions.

Marriage, I thought, sitting poolside, can be

boring—a bit like periodically tossing pennies into a pool, wishing against all hope that someone would read your mind and bring you a snack from the vending machine. Dating is poetry. Marriage is a novel. There are times, maybe years, that are all exposition.

Based on how we met, I believed that with Neal I would never be bored. Anthony, my roommate in Austin—where I was loitering, post-college, and writing about culture for the *Austin Chronicle*—brought home a flyer for a show in the park. It was the photocopy of a driver's license with writing around it explaining that the man in the picture would be performing at a gazebo downtown. He was six foot one and thin and wore glasses and looked a bit like my celebrity crush Crispin Glover.

My roommate and I went to the show. Neal was performing with three of his friends, one friend's son, and a much older man whom I mistook for someone in the show but would later learn was a local drunk who had wandered onstage. Neal read minutes from an instant-messenger conversation he'd had at work, sang songs, played noise music, told a story using sock puppets, and landed some very funny jokes.

Anthony and I laughed a lot, and not only because we felt an obligation as the only people in the audience. I experienced something at that show I've felt few times in my life: I was shocked. Growing up in 1980s Manhattan, I saw so much debauchery that I considered myself unshockable. But watching Neal, I thought, *I've never met anyone like this before.* This was followed hard upon by another thought: *I want to know everything about him.*

I told my editor at the paper that I thought Neal would make a great profile. He was twenty-five and had done forty fully original shows in one year while working a regular job and running with a group of other office workers and at least one small child. He was either a genius or crazy, and either way, he would make an interesting story.

"Okay," my editor said, looking at me over his glasses, "just don't be alone with him."

I interviewed Neal for what became a very long article. Within weeks we were living together.

Neal grew up in a tiny Texas town, playing drums in the high school band and winning a rap contest at the Tyler mall. He grew up going to church three times a week. For a while, cult leader David Koresh lived down the road. A target for law enforcement because of his long hair and general punk appearance, Neal once came close to being shot by police officers when he went to check on his drum kit at a storage unit late at night.

At eighteen, he had a baby with his high

school girlfriend, and they got married. All he ever wanted was to be an artist and a musician, so he found ways to do that even when he was delivering pizzas. A disturbing number of his former classmates are dead or in jail—one was shot by a repo man, others put in prison for robbing the movie theater where they worked. When the survivors have class reunions, they give only a day's notice because no one but Neal lives more than an hour away.

We left Austin together and moved to New York, where he has continued to do shows, only now they are at hip theaters in Manhattan. And yet it's an illusion that the profusion of excitement with which we've surrounded ourselves could inoculate us fully against the boredom of dailiness. For while Neal is a lunatic whose shows are controlled mayhem, he also sulks if I forget to take the chicken out of the freezer in time for it to defrost before dinner.

Our marriage has had hours, days, weeks, and months that I would characterize as boring.

These boring parts come in many forms. There is the boredom of responsibility: crafting a budget, planning meals, arranging child care, cleaning.

"What are you doing?" Neal asked once when he caught me on the floor sorting Playmobil pieces from Legos.

"A dramatization," I said, *"of why there are no Great American Novels by women."*

There is the boredom of knowing what to expect.

"Every time," Neal said, sighing, *"every single time you go to fade the radio to the back of the car so only the boy can hear it, you press the same wrong buttons in the same wrong sequence."*

"Yeah," I said, *"but now I do it faster."*

There is the boredom of other people's needs, their feelings, their annoying habit of being right.

"You broke the bathroom faucet, but I know you'll find some way to blame me for it," Neal said, correctly.*

At such times, when it feels that we have each other all sized up, it's hard not to long for a new mystery to solve. Why keep doing the same jigsaw puzzle, over and over and over again?

Forsaking all others means going deep with one person—exhaustingly deep. Sometimes, listening to Neal chatter on, trying not to react defensively, failing, I feel crushed by the sameness, like I've landed upon a shrill TV show and there's no way to change channels.

Other men, I think at such moments, *wouldn't care if I broke a faucet.* And if they did, I could

---

* It was his fault, because he didn't stop me from breaking it.

find someone else, leapfrogging from one lily pad of tolerance to the next. Or I could be alone, in which case I could break all my faucets and no one would say a thing.

A few years into our marriage, Neal and I hit a particularly dreary patch of plot development. I was working full-time at a job I'd grown to hate. Neal was touring but making little money. Our toddler was opening and closing drawers. He was so cute, and we loved him so much, and yet so much of his care involved repetition. (Fortunately, with *Dora the Explorer* on, no one can hear you scream.) Neal thought I should be making more time for him, which I found infuriating because I thought he should be thinking about how he could make more money, not about what movie we should go see.

So it should not have been a surprise, though it was, when one day, while Oliver was in his weekly split second of preschool and I was getting dressed to go to a meeting, Neal told me he had feelings for another woman. When he said her name, I flinched. I knew her. She was pretty and familiar. I'd never been jealous of her, and now I felt like a fool. I'd thought I'd known his mind and heart through and through; had I known him at all?

"You *what?*" I screamed. I cried so hard I could barely breathe. On the way to my meeting, I tried to fix my makeup, but my face was so puffy it was useless. When I got to the office, I lied and said it was allergies. Halfway through the meeting, I excused myself to visit the bathroom, where I cried some more.

Monogamy is, by definition, sameness. Other people provide a reliable escape from the boring parts of the story. In the song "Reasons I Cheat," Randy Travis lists indignities: a tough day at work, wounded pride, aging. This woman Neal had developed feelings for, she told him he was great. I probably hadn't said that to him in a while.

A couple of years ago, a man from the middle of the country, having read something I'd written in the *New York Times*, sent me a long e-mail about affairs he'd had in the course of his fifteen-year marriage. A physical affair had done little damage, but an emotional one had proved a torment, estranging him from his wife and hurting the other woman, whom he referred to as "J."

"What did I want from J?" he asked.

> I wasn't available for marriage. Not to be her boyfriend. But to be something. I thought, how nice. We can do this. We can recognize we can never be together.

But maybe we can carve out a space for this in our lives. We can go on secret dinners. We can maybe hold each other in the parking lot. Maybe kiss. Share sweet emails. Enjoy our emotional connection. And then go back to our lives. But of course this seems silly to write. How can you stay only a little bit in love?

When Neal told me about the other woman, I threw him out, telling him to sort out his feelings somewhere else. He went to stay with his best bachelor friend, and he also went, curiously, to talk to my father. "You could leave," my father told him, "but you wouldn't fix anything. Wherever you go, there you are. You would just have different problems. Are the problems you have now so bad that any other problems would be better?"

Sex advice columnist Dan Savage says that everyone talks in their wedding vows about how they would "walk through fire" or "take a bullet" for each other without realizing that more often than not, the bullet and the fire is your spouse saying to you, "I have feelings for another person" or "I slept with someone else." Many of us who have been through this would prefer a literal bullet to the metaphorical one. (Dan Savage and his husband, taking the approach that the best defense is a good offense, have rejected the ideal of perfect monogamy and consider themselves "monogamish.")

"I still love you," Neal said after telling me about that other woman. "I love our life together. I don't want to leave you. I just don't know what to do with these feelings for her."

"Kill them with fire," I suggested.

In 2012, the second ex-wife of conservative presidential candidate Newt Gingrich said that he'd asked her for an open marriage after revealing an affair. When he was questioned about this in a debate, he responded as though auditioning for the Broadway company of a play called *How Dare You, Sir?* He condemned the open marriage rumor, though he did not deny having had a six-year-long clandestine affair— evidently less of an embarrassment.

At a library sale, I discovered a long out-of-print marriage advice book originally published in 1938, and it had one of the most reasonable passages I've ever read about infidelity:

> I am stating that emotional entanglements of greater or less severity (not necessarily culminating in technical infidelity) are very apt to occur in the best-regulated

of marriages, and that there is no ideal way of handling them. Monogamy and freedom, concealment and frankness, all lead to unhappy consequences. The discussion is gloomy, however, only if you demand of marriage a vapid perfection. Gliding slowly along smooth unfrequented city avenues in a closed limousine saves you the bumps and dangers of the open highway, but it's not much fun. If we want the flavor and richness of a real marriage in a real world, we have to accept jolts and risks as part of our experience. There is no escape from the complicated joys and sorrows of marriage. We must accept the jangling, painful aspects of a relationship along with the harmonious intimacy. A good marriage is none the worse for periods of jealousy and resentment and struggle. The grave danger of most extramarital relationships, platonic or not, is that we take them too seriously. The motorist is so disturbed by occasional rough roads that he renounces his whole journey, so appalled by a bashed-in fender that he refuses to drive a car again.

Reliable infidelity statistics are notoriously difficult to come by, but studies suggest that at least one in ten, and probably far more, married people cheat. I've begun to think that being good at monogamy—an ability to accept same-ness—isn't a trait, like green eyes; it's a skill, like playing a sport. Some are born with an aptitude; others cultivate one or give themselves permission not to. Some people never look at another person. Others sleep with everything that moves.

Neal and I have found ourselves in the middle—not that we have the much-maligned "open marriage." Actually, scratch that. I'd argue that everyone who leaves the house has an open marriage. It's just a question of *how* open: What about flirting? Watching porn? Friendships with members of the opposite sex?

If marriages exist on a monogamy spectrum between totally closed and totally open, with 0 being never leaving each other's side or looking at another person, even on a screen, and 5 being extended romantic and sexual affairs with many other people, I'm by nature a somewhat flirty but reliably faithful 1–2.

For a time, Neal thought it might make him feel less guilty if I occasionally fooled around with other people. I considered this a lousy idea until I found myself attracted to someone else, at which point I thought he was a genius and engaged in some 3-zone behavior. This was followed by a chaos-fleeing period of 0-ness.

Many of my friends fall into the 0–1 range. They seem neither to be tempted nor to stir up temptation in others. They admit to me that they have opted out of that side of life, a choice some telegraph by wearing sandals with wool socks, like so many Trappist monks. At times, I've envied them their placidity. But then they tell me that they don't have much going on at home sexually, and that sometimes they miss it.

"Paradoxically," says renowned sex therapist Esther Perel, "the things that nurture love are sometimes the very same ones that flatten desire. . . . Family life wants consistency, repetition, routine; and the erotic thrives on the unpredictable, novelty, and the unexpected."

I've noticed that Neal and I need some distance to feel attraction. If we're too connected, there's no space to bridge with desire. If we're too far apart, we become estranged. I've begun to suspect that, regardless of what women's magazines tell us, there might be no perfect way to reach peak sexiness and perfect security simultaneously, that marriage might just involve finding and refinding our own balance between boredom and jealousy, safety and danger.

One woman I met who lives in California and has been married for fourteen years started out her marriage in the 3 zone. When she and her husband were first together, they would sometimes flirt or even make out with other people.* As their marriage changed, that became less okay with her, something she realized when he kissed a libertine friend of theirs: "Before we had kids, it would have turned me on that he made out with a friend of ours at a party. But after. . . . What works the first couple of years might not work once you have kids."

Ultimately, though, she wound up grateful for the disruption: "I realized I wasn't giving my husband what he needed—being a new mother and all that, I was paying a lot more attention to the baby than to him. I realized, *I want to be the person to make my husband feel good.*" After Neal's affair, I felt something like that too, once I got over the shock. It made me sad that he'd been lonely, and it made me face the reality that I'd been lonely too.

An acquaintance of mine and his wife are 5's. They both sometimes sleep with other people, together or apart. "From the start, that was the spirit of our relationship," he said, "a playfulness, and not wanting to hold each other back." He described what he felt a couple needed for this to succeed:

---

* Inspiring just the right amount of jealousy is a time-tested strategy for marital satisfaction, confirmed in independent clinical trials by the *Kama Sutra*'s author and by Beyoncé, as in her club track/white paper "Freakum Dress."

People act like having an open relationship means no boundaries, but really it
involves more boundaries, because you
have to talk all the time to make it work.
There is this idea of "compersion." It's
the idea that it's possible, if you really
love someone, to not be threatened by
their sexual feelings for other people
but to enjoy them. It's a silly word and
comes out of a hippie commune [the free-
love Kerista Commune in San Francisco,
which lasted from 1971 to 1991], but I
think there's something to it. It's kind of
like lascivious empathy. I've felt it. It is
possible to sort of flip jealousy and to take
pleasure in their pleasure.

I'm nowhere near this evolved. When I think
about Neal kissing someone else, I want to start
knocking things off tables. When I think about
myself kissing someone else, I get a thrill. That's
the opposite of lascivious empathy: an anxious
double standard.

Having a very open marriage worked for this
man and his wife for a long time. "It was how
we got together—having adventures—and we
carried it into our marriage," he told me. "We
slept with other people separately and together.
We talked about it, and it made us closer and our

marriage hotter. There were no secrets." Once they had a baby, though, they were spending less and less time together and more and more either with the baby or out in the world alone. "Raising a child can be so isolating," he said. He and his wife were living on parallel tracks.

One day she found a text on his phone from another woman and confronted him about it. Secrecy wasn't part of the arrangement.

"Well, you're having an affair, too," he said. "I know you are."

She admitted it, and they had a huge fight.

"But it was the best thing that could have happened," he said. "Yelling was so much better than lying in bed silent all that time. I felt like I hadn't looked at her for *years*. The next morning, things started getting better, and now they are really great. These Zen masters I met told me that you have to accept the other person one hundred percent, that all fights come from nonacceptance."

Another man I know who has been in the 5 zone told me he'd always prided himself on the sexual openness of his marriage but had recently had an epiphany about the value of the boring parts:

> My best friend's father died suddenly. He was sixty-one and healthy and then one day he woke up, started to say something

to his wife, and fell over, dead. I went to the funeral. A thousand people came. And all these people kept coming up to my friend, saying, "I knew your father for ten years," or five, or twenty, "and he changed my life." All these stories about things he had done for them. He'd been with his wife since they were nineteen. Everyone loved them. They raised this amazing family and helped so many people. Marriage was a collaboration that let them do all these things for other people, that let them find their purpose. And I went home to my wife and I said, "That is the life I want. And we are not going to get there the way we are going, because you with these other men—it dominates my thoughts."

Recently, I found myself doing yard work for the first time in my life. I learned that the way to take care of a tree is to prune back the little shoots and scraggly branches so that the nutrients will go instead toward the rest of the tree, making it stronger. Perhaps avoiding affairs is a little like pruning back a tree to help it grow. If you're fooling around too much, your marriage might make a pretty hedge, but it will never be an oak. Friends and colleagues can't take refuge beneath a shrub.

"When people are married," one friend said, "and they zoom in and out of other people's lives while staying married, they end up hurting others. I think it happens every day, these infidelities, but there is a cost."

Neal stopped seeing the other woman. We talked about it ad nauseam. He suffered. I suffered. She probably suffered, too, and eventually I found myself feeling pity for her. Some friends told me I should leave Neal, saying I deserved someone who would never look at another woman. If such a man existed, though, I doubted I would want him.

I also had to admit that temptation was the least surprising thing that could have happened that year—a year when we were both working a lot and we had a little kid and were apart so often. (I was let go from my job, the one paying most of our bills and providing health insurance, soon after Neal revealed his affair. I think we skipped the Christmas card that year.)

What's more, I knew firsthand how such a thing could happen. When I was living with Neal in New York before we got married, I had a male best friend at work. We had a flotilla of inside jokes, nicknames for our co-workers, and a habit of e-mailing each other all day, every day. We were reading books and listening to songs and watching movies the other had recommended.

We almost never spent time together outside the office, but during work hours we were an army of two.

Then, one night, after work and a couple of drinks, we kissed. And despite how much I'd wanted it to happen, I was caught off guard by its intensity—it was a time-stops, rest-of the-world-melts-away kiss. I'd been looking at him out of the corner of my eye for months, and now here I was staring at him close-up, my hand touching his scratchy face. He became, in an instant, warm and three-dimensional. The transformation was so startling it was like that cartoon where an ordinary frog suddenly sports a cane and top hat and breaks into song.

I was so dazed by that kiss that for minutes I was able to forget there would be consequences. If the kiss had been worse—sloppy, drunken, forgettable—maybe we could have stayed friends. Instead, it alerted us to what roiled beneath the surface of our office banter. It was as though we'd started a garden with our eyes closed and opened them to find it thick with plants. No one else, I realized, would ever quite understand this. Love and sex: they're the ultimate inside joke.

"Just what the hell is your plan here?" Neal asked when I admitted to the kiss.

I had no plan. I'd hoped, vaguely, that I'd be able to keep them both close. Now I was mortified to realize how reckless I'd been. Neal wanted to marry me. He'd believed in us having our own friends, even thought flirting was fine, but he drew the line at my having a boyfriend at work.

His request that I break the friendship off was not unreasonable, but it proved more painful than I'd anticipated. When I pulled away, my friend was furious. And without his amusing, seductive e-mails to sustain me, I began to find that workplace intolerably lonely. I was relieved to get an offer for another job, though I remained heartsick. For years, I hoped I would run into that man on the subway. I imagined I saw him in crowds.

These days, I don't enjoy crushes as much as I used to. That's not how I want to be with other people—selfish, confusing, greedy. I want to be better than that. In her story "Floating Bridge," Alice Munro writes about times "when anything you look at is just a peg to hang the unruly sensations of your body on, and the bits and pieces of your mind." These other men—did I ever really see them? Or were they just projection screens onto which I could shadow-puppet my own desires?

Besides, trying to have fun but not too much fun can be exhausting, like playing the game Operation, where you can extract the prize only if you don't hit any of the sensors on all sides. Maybe more than Operation it's like Russian roulette, because for every five times an extramarital flirtation makes you feel extra alive, there's one crush that kills you.

"Every married woman I know has suffered those unspoken devastations," a friend of mine told me the other day, recalling a moment in her marriage when she was smiling at her husband and doing the dishes but could think of nothing but whether the phone in her pocket would ping with a response from another man. "Everyone talks about what crushes do to a marriage, whether they strengthen it or weaken it or whatever, but no one talks about what it does to *us,* to have that connection and then lose it. It's brutal. And you're all alone in it. Because what are you going to do—ask your husband to comfort you?"

"Marriage involves more suffering than most of modern American life," the poet Sparrow told me. "That's why so many escape it. It's kind of crazy to shop at Target, watch Netflix, drive a Honda, and still have a husband—just like females did in the eleventh century. It's a completely antiquated setup, but no one can think of another one. Or, rather, lots of people can think of many other ones, and they all seem to work well for about two and a half years. Then they collapse."

A few years ago, I made fast friends with a man at a work conference in Florida. We snuck out of a tedious lecture together and drove to a mansion and park called Vizcaya. It was raining, and we walked through the gardens, looking at the plants and out at the ocean and talking as though we'd known each other forever. We sent another conference friend, marooned in the lecture hall, a photo of ourselves smiling in ponchos in the rain. She texted back, "Did you elope?"

Then, because we're both married to other people, we never saw each other again. Now that magical day feels like a waste, like I did job training for a position I'll never take. Worse, I can't turn to Neal and say, "Remember all those giant urns at Vizcaya? So many urns!" I can't talk to anyone about the urns.

"One time when I was seven or eight, I was at Chuck E. Cheese's with my parents," Neal tells me, "feeling totally secure and happy. I was chattering away, and then I got up to go to the bathroom and I came back and sat down still rambling and then I looked up and realized that the people at the table weren't my parents. I'd sat down at the wrong table. I screamed. And that's how my affair felt when I realized what was going on. I looked up and I'd been talking to this other person who wasn't you and I felt terrified."

. . .

The other day, I called Neal from the street, dying to talk to him. "Remember when we moved to this neighborhood," I said when he picked up, "and rented movies at the Smokiest Movie Rental Place in the World? The woman who ran it is still alive! I just passed her on the street!"

Another time, we took Oliver to Disney World and moved according to an elaborate crowd-thwarting strategy I'd culled from the Internet, epitomized by the battle cry "Run to Dumbo!" We didn't wait in any lines. It was the greatest tactical success of my life. "Run to Dumbo!" has served as a family mantra ever since.

That, for me, may be the most persuasive argument for monogamy: it lets you keep all your inside jokes in one place.

A man I know who divorced his wife of fifteen years dated for just a year before marrying again; he is in his fifteenth year of that second marriage. "I thought I would like being single more than I did," he said. "It was like the movie *Home Alone*. At first, it was great. Then it really wasn't." This time around, he's grateful for boredom, seeing it as a challenge rather than a burden: "When you're bored, you're forced to figure things out, to be creative."

• • •

The other day on a city sidewalk, I saw a little boy approach an open fire hydrant. He kept putting his hand in the stream of water over and over again, shrieking with delight each time. His mother looked intensely bored. My heart went out to her. And yet I thought: *I would give every cent I have to spend one more hour with Oliver at that age.*

I try to remember that during the hours I spend throwing coins to him in the pool: how this will feel years later, when he's taller than me and lives on his own. Probably it will feel like nursing does in my memory—like a Madonna and Child fresco illuminated by divine light, rather than a bleary task bathed in the glow of a TV showing the Mets squandering an early lead.

Back then, a labor and delivery nurse explained that breast milk starts out weak and sugary but turns less sweet and more filling—the baby gets dessert first. In marriage, too, I've begun to suspect, the boring later phase nourishes more than the rapture of new love.

Eighteen hours after a discussion about car insurance so boring I wanted to lie down under the collision-damage-waivered wheels, Neal and I found ourselves at a minor-league baseball game. Oliver kept running to the parking lot with the other kids to chase foul balls. As Neal

55

and I sat on the bleachers, everything seemed to make us laugh, from the five-slot hitter's use of the walk-up song "Beast of Burden," which we translated as "No, really, don't count on me to get you home," to the giant cups of ice served with tiny bottles of wine at the concession stand. I felt happy and free and weirdly, dopily in love. Exposition establishes the plot. The boring parts don't last forever. In retrospect, they aren't even boring.

TOAST 3

Containing Multitudes

Marriage is people.
—Maurice Lamm,*The Jewish Way
in Love and Marriage*, 1980

For a week this summer, I wore a tight-bodiced, large-sleeved, floor-length pioneer dress covered with a handmade Red Cross apron, my hair piled on top of my head. I bandaged scrapes with gauze, felt sweaty foreheads to check for fever, and when a child fell and knocked out a baby tooth while playing Ante-I-Over, I put him on the nurse's cot with an old adventure book called *The Coral Island* and a rag cooled in the stream.

"Miss Cook," a little girl in braids and a gingham frock asked me, "could you help me across the road?"

"Nurse Cook," a little boy in overalls and bare feet said, pointing at another child, "he hurt his elbow."

This scenario came about like everything interesting does: completely at random. Oliver had wanted to go to the old-timey camp near his grandparents' house; the only way I could get him off the waiting list was by agreeing to renew my CPR certification and volunteering as the camp nurse. Watching the old-timey children make cornhusk dolls and blackberry ink, play Hoop and Stick, Corncob Darts, and Maypole, I had time to reflect on how we can end up all sorts of places we never thought we would, filling all manner of unlikely roles—even, sometimes, a nineteenth-century nurse named Miss Ruth Cook.

"He's not the man I married," one friend recently gave as her reason for wanting out of her marriage.

"She didn't change and I did" was another's.

So often, too, I hear the no-fault version: "We grew apart."

Feeling oppressed by change or lack of change: it's a tale as old as time. At some point in a marriage, each partner is guaranteed to change. They evolve from the person who stood at the altar into someone new. Sometimes, they become insufferable—a religious fanatic, a militant vegan, a Civil War reenactor (or, worse, all three).

A letter to an advice column from the 1940s reads: "When I look at him I notice only how fat and bald he has got, and how tired I am of hearing him tell about what happened at the office. I don't bother to cook extra dishes for him. . . . And as for jealousy of other women, why, he can hire 'Miss America' for his secretary for all I care."

I've read similar testimonials from just about every era in recorded history. Medieval texts raise this grievance to the level of fetish. A French satire called *The Fifteen Joys of Marriage*, dating to the early 1400s, ends every chapter with a variation on this line: "For he is in the trap and there he will be always and will end his days miserably." (In modern times, we whine less poetically.)

What I see happening with many of my divorcing friends is that they feel betrayed by change. They fall in love with one person, and when that person doesn't seem familiar anymore, they feel he or she has violated the marriage contract. They take their feelings of distaste and estrangement as a sign that the marriage is over, that either too much change or not enough has come to topple the relationship like a baby with a stack of blocks.

And yet I've begun to wonder if perhaps the problem isn't change itself but, rather, our susceptibility to what's been called the "end of history" illusion. "Human beings are works in progress that mistakenly think they're finished," says Harvard professor Daniel Gilbert, whose study subjects said they'd changed hugely in the years prior but insisted they were done and in the future wouldn't change anymore.

A couple of years ago, I wrote a book about the street I grew up on. In the course of doing interviews, I listened to one person after another swear up and down that the street was a shadow of its former self, that all the good businesses had closed and all the good buildings had been knocked down and all the good people had died. Each resident took it personally, talking as though the street were a fickle lover who had abandoned them.

But I began to notice something: everyone's golden era was different. Some said the city was at its best in the 1940s. Others said the 1960s. Some said the 1980s. And I recognized a trend. The year everyone said the street was best was the year they felt most alive and excited about the world—usually when they were about nineteen.

Nostalgia—which generally goes hand in hand with resentment toward change—is a natural human impulse. And yet being happy with the same person forever requires finding ways to be happy with different versions of that person, and avoiding panic when the person you're with becomes someone you dislike. Maybe you'll enjoy the next person they become. Maybe the person you're on your way to becoming will like this new partner better.

Because I like to fix broken things as quickly and as shoddily as possible (Neal describes my renovation aesthetic as "*Little Rascals* Club-house"), I frequently receive the advice "Don't just do something, stand there." Underreacting might be the best stance when confronted by too much or too little change. Whether we want people to stay the same or not, time will give us change in abundance.

At the old-timey camp, Oliver's "schoolhouse name" was James Boggs, making his camp sister Callie Boggs, a tiny little girl in a perfectly tailored Laura Ingalls Wilder dress, with her dark hair pulled back into a ponytail. The pair of them, thrown together by the name draw, developed a filial affinity and a shared obsession with a game called the Graces, which involves using sticks to throw a wooden hoop back and forth. I e-mailed the town historian to ask if he knew anything about Ruth Cook or James Boggs, and he told me this: "James Boggs had the farm on Boggs Road, just up from the school. He was born in 1884 and was married three times and had six children by his first two wives. His sister Callie was born in 1883 and married Milt Hastings when she was 67 years old in 1950. She died in 1966." He even had a photo of them. But he knew nothing about me, Ruth.

And so I made her up. Descended from the explorer Captain Cook, Ruth became a nurse in the country in order to escape her adventurous family. But she could not contradict her nature, and so even here she fell in with a crowd of suffragettes and anarchists. During this period of time, even being seen at the ice cream parlor in town was grounds for dismissal by the school board, so Ruth had to hide her illicit activities, particularly her affair with a time-traveling musician named Billy England. (One day while I was at camp, Neal on a whim recorded an entire album as a character by that name and tried to pass it off to me as the unreleased studio tape of a late-1980s singer-songwriter. There are a lot of songs about miners and Margaret Thatcher. It worked for me on many levels.)

That summer was full of surprises. Not only did I become an old-timey nurse and Neal a British protest singer, but we also became home owners. Every time we visited his grandparents that year, Oliver would note that a pretty blue house near them was still for sale.

We weren't in the market for a house, though Neal and I had been dreaming of real estate. Our aforementioned apartment in the city is five hundred square feet. Neal, Oliver, and my twenty-two-year-old stepson Blake are all inconveniently tall. Even Ginny the Turtle had recently required an upgrade to a larger tank; she now occupied a quarter of our shelf space.

I got out my phone and looked up the listing. I did a double take, then handed the phone to Neal.

"Why does it cost so little?" he said. "Is it a fake house, like a movie set?" (This giant house cost a tiny fraction of what a closet would be in Brooklyn.)

So now we own a house. Oliver commandeered a little room under the stairs and turned it into a nook called the Lego Office. We have a basement in which to put all our stuff, so now our tiny apartment in the city is less cluttered and, therefore, less claustrophobic. We bought furniture and had pictures framed and set up a badminton net in the backyard and got pretty good at badminton. We marveled at the change that had come over us. Who were these backyard-grilling, property-tax-paying, shuttlecock-batting people we had become overnight? Fifteen years ago, when we met, Neal wasn't a man who would delight in lawn care; nor was I the kind of person who would have found such a man appealing. And yet here we were, avidly refilling our bird feeder and remarking on all the cardinals.

Neal, in particular, loves everything about the house. I was surprised, because he'd never shown any interest in householding. Once I overheard him heckle an HGTV show: "The *kitchen island* isn't big enough? Go fuck yourself!" But now he had opinions on bookshelves and curtains, and he loved going to the hardware store, and he whistled while he mowed. He was like an alien. But in this new scenario, I was an alien, too. And our alien selves were remarkably compatible.

In college, a friend and I were obsessed with a reality TV show called *Change of Heart*. A couple "at a crossroads in their relationship" would go on the show to explore other options on national TV. The show would pair each person up with their fantasy date. So if the boyfriend was a slob and she wished he were neater, she would get a sexy librarian for her date. If the girlfriend was uptight, he might be paired with an exotic dancer.

Though hardly a scientific study, it often proved weirdly satisfying. I sometimes imagine myself on the *Change of Heart* couch—Neal matched with someone louche like Aubrey Plaza's character on *Parks and Recreation*, me with someone reserved like a *Pride and Prejudice*–era Colin Firth. Though I've also begun to suspect that if you stay together long enough, you wind up seeing your husband or wife as a series of successful and unsuccessful *Change of Heart* contestants.

One seventy-year-old woman I know married a hot young Communist poet fifty years ago.

When the Berlin Wall fell, he felt betrayed by his ideals and became a Republican. He's mellowed now, into a benevolent quasi-Libertarian. Both he and his wife have survived cancer and become grandparents. She has, essentially, been married to three men: a young lefty, a middle-aged conservative, and an apolitical old man—just by sticking around. Today she's almost annoyingly devoted to her husband. "Mom," her daughter tells her, "could you please stop talking about Dad like you're a teenager and he's your biker boyfriend? He's great, sure. Just stop."

"I've had at least three marriages," more than one long-married person has told me. "They've just all been with the same person."

My first husband, Nick, and I met at my first college, in Montreal, when we were nineteen. A college-radio DJ and cultural studies major, he had grown up in suburban Ontario (which, coming from New York City, I found more exotic than his Portuguese heritage). We dated for a few months and then dropped out of school together and drove cross-country. Over the next couple of years, we'd work a series of low-wage jobs and drive a beat-up van and be inseparable. He hadn't dated many people before we got together, and so on the rare occasions when we discussed our potential long-term, he said that he wasn't ready to settle down permanently; one day he would probably need to "sow his wild oats"—a saying I found tacky and a concept I found ridiculous.

"Maybe you found it ridiculous because you'd already done it," says Neal, who spent most of his brief dating years after his teen marriage trapped in various friend zones and so is more sympathetic to Nick's dilemma.

It's true that from ages sixteen to nineteen, I'd had a lot of boyfriends. But with Nick, I became happily domestic. We adopted cats together. I had changed in such a way that I had no problem being with just one person. And yet I felt like he had one foot out the door with his one-day-I'll-have-to-roam talk.

When we got married at the courthouse so he could get his green card, I didn't feel different the next day. We kept falling asleep each night with *Politically Incorrect* on in the background and our cats sleeping at our feet. We told anyone who asked that the marriage was no big deal, just a formality so the government wouldn't break us up. But when pressed, it was hard to say what differentiated us from the truly married, beyond the absence of a party. When I grew depressed a few months later, I decided that he and our pseudo-marriage were part of the problem. After three years of feeling like the more committed person, I was done. I asked him to move out. When he left, I felt sad, but also thrilled by the prospect of dating again. A couple of years and several musicians later, I met Neal.

Recently, I asked Nick if we could talk. We hadn't spoken in a decade or so. He lives in London now, so we Skyped. I saw that he looked almost exactly like he had at twenty-two, though he'd grown a long beard. We had a pleasant conversation. Finally, I asked him if he thought it counted, our early, ambivalent marrying.

"Yeah," he said. "I think it counts."

We were married, just not very well. To borrow a phrase from the priest who married me and Neal, we didn't know why we were there. The marriage didn't mean very much to us, and so when things got rough, we broke up. I'd been too immature to know what I was getting into. I thought passion was the most important thing. When my romantic feelings left, I felt an obligation to follow them out the door. It was just like any breakup, except that because we'd been married there was some extra paperwork.

Nick now works at a European arts venue. He's unmarried. I wouldn't have predicted his life or his facial hair. I don't regret our breakup, but if we'd stayed married, I think I would have liked this version of him.

Neal says that one thing he likes about owning a house away from the city is that it lets him imagine us living an alternate, country life: "I'd cover songs like 'Margaritaville' at the local hotel, and you'd become a nurse at the hospital. And every night you'd come home, kick off your Crocs, and say, 'Oof, my dogs are barkin'!' "

This fantasy is ludicrous. I have neither the temperament nor the academic prowess for medicine, and once I worked at *Vogue*, so if I ever wear Crocs, I fear my former bosses will come to my house and set them on fire. Perhaps because of the fantasy's absurdity, it has captured my family's imagination. "Remember, Mom," says Oliver, "how you're going to get a job in the hospital? And every night you'll come home and kick off your Crocs? And you'll say, 'Oof, my dogs are barkin'?' " Then he dissolves in laughter. Every once in a while, Neal puts pale blue scrubs and yellow Crocs in our Amazon cart and waits for me to notice.

The red-haired schoolmarm at the old-timey camp moved back and forth between the present and the past with inspiring good humor.

"What's that?" a child said, spotting her trying to take a photo with her iPhone of the children eating their wax-paper and dishcloth-wrapped lunches.

"Oh, just a mirror," the schoolmarm replied breezily.

"What's that?" a child asked, seeing a car on the road.

"Hmm," the schoolmarm said, squinting, "it appears to be a horseless carriage from the future. Don't go near it, children."

She acknowledged reality while keeping the children's imaginations firmly in the year 1900. We discussed William McKinley's reelection campaign and his promising vice presidential running mate, Teddy Roosevelt. The older students fetched water from a spring. Only there was no spring—the teacher had hidden a plastic water cooler in the woods, and they used that to fill the pail.

"The heat's supposed to break later," the schoolmarm said. "Nurse Cook told me. How did you know that, Nurse Cook?"

"*The Farmer's Almanac*?" I said.

"Yes," she said. "Nurse Cook always reads *The Farmer's Almanac*. Thank goodness for Benjamin Franklin."

When I contributed grapes to the morning snack, she asked where I'd gotten them. "I have a vineyard?" I said. This prompted peals of delighted laughter.

"Good luck with that," she said. (Our frequently freezing region of the Catskills isn't exactly the Italian countryside.)

We teachers and students were playing at being one thing without ever hiding the fact that it was a game. An ability to operate on multiple levels benefits a marriage. We do well to remember that what we do for a living, what hobbies we prefer, what we weigh, what kind of mood we're in—it's most likely temporary.

My hair is long and blond now. When Neal and I met, I'd kept it dyed black and cut it to my chin. When I took to bleaching it myself, it was often orange, because I didn't know what I was doing. Now I weigh about 160 pounds. When I left the hospital after being treated for a burst appendix and didn't want to even look at food, I weighed 140. When I was nine months pregnant and starving every second, I weighed 210. I've been everything from a size 4 to a size 14. I've been the life of the party and I've been a drag, broke and loaded, clinically depressed and radiantly happy. Spread out over the years, I'm a harem.

"Is it weird that I think it's kind of exciting that now I get to experience what it's like to have sex with a fat person—as a fat person?" says a friend who, like her husband, has put on some weight. "Why don't people ever talk about that, how *interesting* it is getting to know this other person's body as well as your own, and to see it through all of its changes? I wish people would stop asking, 'How can I spice things up in the bedroom?' and instead see that the real question is, 'How can I cultivate detachment with regard to my sex life?'"

What is the key, in other words, to caring less—about things like how much sex we're having and whether or not it's the best sex possible? How can we accept that when it comes to our bodies, the only inevitability is change?

One day in the country, Neal and I heard a chipmunk in distress. It had gotten into the house and was hiding under the couch. Every few minutes, the creature let out a high-pitched noise that sounded like a smoke alarm announcing a low battery. I tried to sweep it out the door to safety with a broom, but it kept running back at my feet.

"Wow, you're dumb," I said to the chipmunk.

"I got this," Neal said, mysteriously carrying a salad bowl. "Shoo it out from under there."

I did, and the chipmunk raced through the living room.

Neal, like an ancient discus thrower, tossed the bowl in a beautiful arc. It landed perfectly around the scampering creature. Neal slid a piece of cardboard under the bowl and carried the chipmunk out into the bushes, where he set it free.

"That was really impressive," I said.

"I know," he said.

To feel awed by a man I thought I knew through and through—it's a shock when it happens

71

after so many years. And a boon. That one fling of a salad bowl probably bought us at least five more years of marriage. As did the Billy England album featuring my new favorite song, "Council Tenants—Right to Buy, Right to Die."

Pope Francis once told a group of engaged couples that married life is about two people gradually changing each other for the better. He said marriage is creative, "a craftsman's task, a goldsmith's work, because the husband has the duty of making the wife more of a woman and the wife has the duty of making the husband more of a man. . . . One day you will walk along the streets of your town and the people will say: 'Look at that beautiful woman, so strong!' 'With the husband that she has, it's understandable!' "

One of the last days of camp, it rained. The children stayed inside, doing crafts and memorizing poems. Oliver was assigned the part of Walt Whitman's "I Hear America Singing" about workers harmonizing at the end of a long day. I lay on the cot of my nurse's station and read a book. Every once in a while, one of the older students would show up and ask me to listen to them recite pieces of "Hiawatha," but for most of the morning I just lay there eating graham crackers and thinking about my double life. On this rainy August day, I had my very own house and family with Neal, and yet I was also an explorer's great-great-great granddaughter and a nurse, with a secret lover named Billy England. And when the school day ended, I could go home to both of them.

TOAST 4

The Truth About Soul Mates

Love is something ideal, marrying is something real, and no one ever confuses the ideal with the real without being punished for it.
—Johann Wolfgang von Goethe, c. 1823

In 1997, soon after Nick and I moved to Austin, Texas, I got a job as a printer at a dating-service photo lab. Along with a few other twenty-somethings perhaps not living their best lives, I printed profile pictures of men and women who were seeking love and fulfillment via a national dating service. Everything was done by mail. Film came in each morning; prints went out each night. On breaks, we sat out back by a sad cactus, smoking and drinking lukewarm coffee.

At our machines, we printed roll after roll of film, making fun of the people in the pictures looking for love in San Diego and Denver. On one wall of the lab, my bookish colleague Richard and I would tape up our favorites, creating a celebrity look-alike section. In Sharpies on these photos we wrote, "Old Keanu" or "That Lady from *Who's the Boss?*" The categories with the most images were "Janet Reno" and "Magnum P.I." We made decks of cards out of the proofs and played a twisted version of Memory with them after hours.

Another co-worker, Stephen, and I especially enjoyed the photos of people that appeared in October. Why they thought it was appropriate to show up to their photo shoots wearing Halloween garb we never knew, but we were grateful. We printed hundreds of copies of one frumpy, gray-haired woman who had chosen two portraits of herself in cat makeup for her profile. In one, she was smiling; in the other, frowning. We called these photos Happy Kitty and Grumpy Kitty, and we hid them all over the lab. If I went to make a cup of coffee, I would find that the filters had been replaced by a stack of Grumpy Kitties. If Stephen reached for a book of negatives on an upper shelf, Happy Kitties showered onto his head.

An obstacle to our delight in these games was our boss, Peter, a perpetually annoyed, joy-killing Huskers fan who not only made us take down our celebrity wall and turn down our music (usually the Replacements) but who even made us compete at games like ring toss and golf putting for Christmas bonuses. We wouldn't have minded, except that the receptionist, who had otherwise distinguished herself only by calling in sick from grief when Chris Farley died, surprised us all by exhibiting the focus of a ninja master. She annihilated us in every game, clearing a small fortune and leaving the rest of us with barely enough to let us get drunk on Shiner Bock after work.

Then, out of nowhere, Peter died. We heard he was driving when he had a heart attack and crashed. At the funeral, we sat in a back row of the newly built church while a preacher who seemed to be just out of seminary described a man who bore no resemblance to the man we'd worked for.

"Peter was generous, and kind, and loving," he said, causing us to elbow one another. One of his friends said, "Peter and I used to go out on his boat. I don't know whose boat I'm going to go out on now." He looked searchingly around the room.

In an unintentional boat segue, the preacher said that Peter's fiancée wanted everyone to listen to "their song." On the loudspeaker, the silence was broken by "My Heart Will Go On" from *Titanic*. With characteristic viciousness, one co-worker joked that this signaled that the fiancée would be on the rebound at the reception—a cocktail hour, by the way, with a cash bar.

Everything about that workplace was unromantic, ungenerous, and unloving. We made fun of the people in the pictures for being desperate, but we were desperate, too. After splitting up with Nick, I went on a tear, careening between an exhilarating awareness of my reawakened sexual power and a deep sense of injustice because those I wanted most were too aloof, and those who wanted me most were too present.

Stephen frequently described to me his sordid exploits with strangers. Richard had sworn off love and sex altogether and turned his apartment into a Spartan den of chore lists. We were deeply flawed, unhappy people with lousy love lives.

Never was that clearer than on days when we were charged with printing photos for "success stories." People who met through the dating service and fell in love were invited to sit for a package of pictures of them together, cuddling and staring into each other's eyes. Looking into our negative carriers at those happy Janet Renos and Magnum P.I.s, seeing how they had looked for and found their soul mates, we knew the joke was really on us.

———————

The best wedding toast I've ever heard was delivered by my cousin Rhoades, who's a few years older than me, at his brother's wedding. It was about the statistical impossibility of soul mates. He calculated the odds of ever finding the one person "meant for you," given the billions of people on the planet, the number of people you're likely to meet in the course of your life, and the fact that in the scheme of human history, none of us stays in a corporeal body for very long. If soul mates are real, statistically speaking you would have to live many thousands of lifetimes without love. Rhoades concluded by saying, "So I think the odds are against your being soul mates, but that doesn't make it less of a miracle that you found each other."

J.R.R. Tolkien, the author of *The Lord of the Rings*, did not live a fantastical life. Orphaned as a child and raised by a local priest, he embraced tradition and academia. He fell in love with a young woman named Edith when they were teenagers, married her as soon as he came of age, supported her and their children in the suburbs as a professor, and remained by her side until she died, at the age of eighty-two.

"Ronald [as he was known] would have to tolerate Edith's absorption in the daily details of life, trivial as they might seem to him," said a biographer. "She would have to make an effort to understand his preoccupation with his books and languages, selfish as it might appear to her."

"Only a *very* wise man at the *end* of his life could make a sound judgment concerning whom, amongst the total possible chances, he ought most profitably to have married," Tolkien wrote in a letter to his son. "Nearly all marriages, even happy ones, are mistakes: in the sense that almost certainly (in a more perfect world, or even with a little more care in this very imperfect one) both partners might have found more suitable mates. But the 'real soul-mate' is the one you are actually married to."

My cousin Jeremy believed in soul mates. He was two years older than me, and my opposite in almost every way. I lived in the city; he lived in the country. I was shy; he was outgoing. I had blond hair; he had brown. I was a good girl; he was a rascal. Growing up, he was the closest thing I had to a brother.

During holidays and summers, we played hide-and-seek, had bottle-rocket fights, and picked leeches off our bodies after swimming. We shared a tree house. We shot skeet in a field. As kids, we watched *The Incredible Hulk*. As tweens, we tried to unscramble the satellite so we could make believe we were viewing a blurry Playboy channel. We played the McDonald's Monopoly sweepstakes like it was our job. We recorded a "radio show" on a cassette player—"This is Twins Radio, coming at you from . . . *upstairs!*"—that featured dreadful Ronald Reagan and Rambo jokes we'd cribbed from *Mad* magazine.

We attended freezing early-morning swim

classes together, to which his big sister grudgingly chauffeured us while blasting Madonna's "Holiday." We took baths together until we were too old to take baths together. When we were teenagers, we got in his car, a wrecked-up Pinto that eventually caught fire, and drove out to remote fields, where we drank warm beer around campfires. And when I was fifteen, I fell in love with one of his friends.

Steve was nineteen. When I looked at him, it was like being caught in a tractor beam. He wore an engineer's cap and had sleepy eyes and John Lennon glasses, and if he had asked me to drop out of high school, marry him, and live in a trailer in the woods, I would not have hesitated for one second.

When I left the living room of some random underfurnished house in which my cousin's friends and I were sitting around smoking too many cigarettes, Steve would come find me. We made out in barns, in hallways, and in his cool old car. We never went further because I was inexperienced and he was considerate, and, looking back, he also probably was not that serious about me, whereas I had never felt so sure of anything in my whole life.

On a road trip in college, Nick and I stopped in to stay with Jeremy in Arizona and found a note saying he was sorry, that he'd left for his own road trip that morning with a woman he'd just met who was his soul mate.

Even though his roommates let me and Nick crash on the kitchen floor, I was mad that Jeremy had bailed on our plans. Here we were suddenly with this group of New Agey southwestern hippies who left all the doors and windows open and who thought it was hilarious and not terrifying when a large, be-fanged, bristly-haired wild beast—as it turned out, an animal called a javelina—wandered into the house in the middle of the night. I was further annoyed because Jeremy's relationship with his soul mate didn't survive. When I reminded him of her some years later, he said, "Who?"

Tolkien and his wife bickered. But friends noted how, in their old age, they functioned as a sort of kindly two-headed creature. One visitor recalled Tolkien discoursing on etymology at the same time that his wife described a grand-child's measles—speaking over each other, but in harmony. On summer evenings, they sat together on their front porch or in their garden, smoking and marveling at how with little in the way of role models, they had created their own happy family.

In that letter to his son, Tolkien blamed the "soul mates" myth on the Romantic chivalric tradition: "Its weakness is, of course, that it began as an artificial courtly game, a way of enjoying love for its own sake. . . . It takes, or at any rate has in the past taken, the young man's eye off women as they are"—that is, "companions in shipwreck not guiding stars."

One fall, a few months into my infatuation with Steve, I was visiting Jeremy and he took me to a house party. Steve was there, but he acted like he didn't even know me. I looked out a window onto a roof where some people were gathered. I saw him canoodling with what appeared to be a short brunette cheerleader.

I wanted to file a complaint with a bureaucratic agency, one that might deluge him with certified letters and tie him up in courts.

"He's my *soul mate,*" I would have written on the triplicate forms, "and so we're supposed to be together forever, or surely we're supposed to get more than a season of making out on the bench seats of his Buick."

I couldn't even plead my case to our friends. First of all, they were *his* friends—other nineteen-year-old men who drove in demolition derbies and tacked *High Times* centerfolds to their bedroom walls. I was just an occasional visitor from the city wearing blackberry lipstick.

My whole romance with Steve had taken place in the literal and figurative dark. I sent him a note, through a friend of mine who knew him from school. He never wrote back. I started to think I'd imagined everything.

"Did Steve ever care about me?" I asked Jeremy.

"Yes, he loved you," Jeremy said. "He just couldn't handle how intense it was."

Jeremy lied to me a lot over the years; this one time I was grateful.

Not long after that, Jeremy got caught with heroin near our apartment in the city. With Lou Reed's "Satellite of Love" playing in the background, Jeremy swore to me that he'd been framed. I didn't believe him. He insisted that if I really cared about him, I would defend him to our parents.

"Okay," I said dramatically, "but if it turns out later that you were lying, I'll never believe you again." He swore up and down. Years later, at Thanksgiving, I made some reference to it and he said, "Oh, yeah, no, I totally bought those drugs." We mostly lost touch after that.

The soul mate ideal appears in Plato's *Symposium*. Zeus, seeking to humble humankind, split us in half, condemning us to wander in search of our other half: "So ancient is the desire of one another which is implanted in us, reuniting our original nature, making one of two, and healing the state of man."

The poet Samuel Taylor Coleridge is credited

with coining the term "soul mate" in English, though he seems to be thinking of the concept more practically. "In order not to be miserable," he tells a young woman contemplating marriage, "you must have a *Soul*-mate as well as a *House* or a *Yoke*-mate."

The former monk Thomas Moore offers a Coleridgean take on soul mates: "If you agree to harbor another person's soul," Moore wrote in 1994, "you are in for a bout with the unknown. Even that person has no idea what is in store for him and where he will be asked to go next. So when we agree to share lives, we are offering to be part of a dynamic, unpredictable adventure."

The summer I was twenty-eight, the phone rang at six a.m. in the loft apartment Neal and I were sharing in Brooklyn. We were a few weeks away from our wedding. I wondered, blearily, if a guest in a different time zone could be calling to change an RSVP. I answered the phone to learn that Jeremy was dead. He had hanged himself.

When I'd seen him in prior years at family functions, he'd had a manic energy. His perpetually wide-open eyes and rictus grin had made him seem like an *Invasion of the Body Snatchers* version of my cousin. But he'd been living with a girlfriend and doing electrical work and in touch with other people in our family, and so I hadn't worried about him too much. Now I felt guilty that I hadn't tried to keep him close.

Neal and I packed our bags and went upstate. At the funeral home, which stood next door to the church where we would marry a month later, we saw him laid out. He looked strange and scary, and like he was holding his breath.

My teenage mind fixated on Truth and Beauty and the Real and other Ideals Requiring Capital Letters. Raised agnostic, I craved some sort of spiritual awakening. At garage sales, I bought books with titles like *Mysticism* or *Into the Unknown*. And I thought a lot about death. Tolkien described death as "the divine paradox." In life, love is flawed. In death, it is perfect. In life, I'd had complicated feelings about Jeremy. Now, I felt nothing but sorrow.

The service was held by a stream on my aunt and uncle's property, in the same spot where they had been married many years before. As they had for my photo-lab boss, the eulogies here seemed to be about someone other than the person I'd known. They described him in generic, touchy-feely terms. I hadn't planned to say anything, but I felt called to speak, like they say people do in Quaker meetinghouses.

"I'm listening to you talk about Jeremy," I said, standing up, "and I think it's nice that you all remember him as such a sweet person. I remember him differently. I loved him, but I can't forget he was also so *bad*."

I mentioned a few of the pranks he'd pulled on me when we were children: he convinced me that there was a ghost lurking in a nearby old foundation, and that there was a mummy inhabiting the locked closet of the room where I slept (or, from then on, did not sleep). Once he shook me awake and dragged me a quarter mile down the road to a field, where he showed me a crop circle and told me an elaborate story about having seen a spaceship land, going so far as to draw pictures of the aliens. (He later confessed that he'd woken before dawn and spent hours riding his bike in circles to make the grass lay down that way.)

I recalled him shooting me with bottle rockets and throwing leeches at me and pushing me out of rubber rafts. What I didn't say but thought was that for as much as I'd loved him, he had been gone from my life for a while. I had missed him, I realized, a lot, and for a long time. Suicide doesn't always happen all at once; sometimes the person leaves the world little by little.

After the service, Neal and I were walking back up to the house for the reception, my high heels sinking into the grass, when Steve, who I hadn't seen or spoken to in a decade, stopped me.

"Hey, Ada," he said, standing there with the eyes and the glasses and the tall, thin body.

"I liked what you said," he told me.

What I would have done for this much attention from him back in high school made me shudder. I would have killed for this. I would still be in jail.

"Thanks," I said. "You guys were always doing stuff like that, but I was still happy you let me hang out with you."

I introduced him to Neal, and he introduced me to his fiancée.

"This is Jeremy's cousin," he said to her. "She and I had a little thing back in the day."

A little thing.

In the midst of death, I felt a rush of joy.

I worried that his fiancée would be annoyed by this talk of our little thing—*our* little thing; our little *thing*—and that her distress would mar my delight. So I said, "Steve's too nice. I was just a kid with a crush on him." Which was true, too.

Neal, amused by my gloating, said, "Well, that must have felt good," as we walked up the hill to the reception.

Was Steve my soul mate? Maybe. But what's that worth in the long run? If we'd moved into a trailer in the woods, like I'd wanted to, so many good things never would have happened to him or to me. If Steve was my soul mate, soul mates are overrated.

● ● ●

A few years after Jeremy died, his parents moved out of the house where they had raised him, where I had spent my childhood summers. One day I had to drop off my parents' car at a repair shop near Ann and Bob's new place, so Oliver and I visited them for lunch. The house was charming—with a jigsaw puzzle in progress on a table and an adored Boston terrier named Pip frolicking around. My aunt and uncle cheerfully bore platters of cold cuts and rolls into the dining room.

Ann and Bob had been frugal and saved for retirement, and now they are enjoying it, with trips around the country and doting on their grandchildren. After a lifetime of beaters, Bob had bought a new car with heated seats. For fun, they'd driven it down to Florida and back.

"You see all these stories of couples that divorce after the death of a child," Ann said when I asked how they'd made it through Jeremy's death. "Fortunately, that wasn't the case for us. We were the opposite. It made us closer. We were in it together. We held each other up. God, I can't imagine going through that alone."

They looked at each other and started trying to pick out what had kept them together. "Respect, I guess?" Ann said. "We're nice to each other. We know now it's not all butterflies and fireworks."

They were quiet for a second, thinking. "Remember when you threw that dish at my head?" Bob asked.

"Right!" Ann said. "I did do that. I don't think I was trying to hit you in the head, though. It shattered against the wall."

What was the fight about?

"He was so stubborn," Ann told me. "Well, he still is. If you tell him you don't like something he's doing, he argues with you, and explains how you're just not looking at it the right way. That used to drive me insane. I just wanted him to hear what I was saying."

She looked over at Bob and then said, "The way I look at it, when you get married, you have these rough edges. Everyone does. And then as you stay together, you wear down each other's rough edges, until they're smooth."

She made a gesture with her hands: first the knuckles clunking against each other, then the palms gliding one over the other. "It's not like we're so much different than we used to be, exactly," she said. "But we've adjusted to each other. We know what to expect, how to work around it. And now when he goes away for even a day or two, I miss him."

This is something I've heard again and again from the long-married.

"He's very efficient," one woman I know said, looking at her husband with so much affection,

I felt like I was intruding. "And I procrastinate. We used to fight about it all the time, but now we just work around each other. He lets me sit there and drink coffee in the morning while he bustles around. When we're on vacation, we spend one day the way he wants to—usually getting up early and driving to every bakery in town—and the next day the way I want to—sleeping in, strolling. We take care of each other. But we had to learn that, how to sync up."

Another friend told me that his tradition-minded parents didn't have much binding them together when they married: "She was Jewish, and he had a good job; that was enough." They struggled while their kids were growing up, resolving to stay together until the nest was empty and then go their separate ways. But something funny happened: by the time the children were grown, neither wanted to leave.

If I try, I can conjure the feeling I had when looking into Steve's eyes back then, watching him move languidly through a run-down college apartment full of smoke, feeling his body pushing into mine against the wall of a barn, smiling out the car window when he reached across the front seat to hold my hand. What I felt then was longing, was wonder, was magical. And yet, considering those moments today, what we had back then seems small.

• • •

Tolkien believed that original sin was responsible for the world's suffering. Of soul mates, Tolkien said, "In such great inevitable love, often love at first sight, we catch a vision, I suppose, of marriage as it should have been in an unfallen world."

Tolkien's "companions in shipwreck" are what my aunt and uncle resembled, standing in their bright kitchen, more wrinkled and weathered than they'd been back when I was a little girl swimming in the pond, hunting for Easter baskets, and watching TV with their son. They'd had the worst thing happen to them, and yet here they were, her giving him a peck as he left for Home Depot. They are the real soul mates, and I don't read books about mysticism anymore.

TOAST 5

Fighting in Rental Cars

To the end, spring winds will sow disquietude, passing faces leave a regret behind them, and the whole world keep calling and calling in their ears. For marriage is like life in this—that it is a field of battle, and not a bed of roses.

—Robert Louis Stevenson,
Virginibus Puerisque, 1881

S o I really like Fleetwood Mac all of a sudden," Neal says as we drive to Gettysburg, Pennsylvania, listening to the classic rock station. "And I was like, 'Why do I like this now?' And then I thought, 'Oh right, I just turned forty.' "

Then Neal tests my musical knowledge.

"Who's this?" he asks, pointing to the radio.

"CCR," I say.

"You always think it's CCR."

"It always is CCR."

"Not this time. Guess again."

"I don't know. The Eagles."

"Ha, nope. It's Boston."

"Okay."

"You can tell it's one of those seventies bands with the place names because of the solos and the changes."

"Now who's this?" Neal asks three minutes later.

"CCR," I say.

Three hours later, we were only halfway there, and the car had become a pit of misery. We'd gotten off at the exit recommended by an app promising to identify exits with the best gas, food, and lodging options. We had waited for this embarrassment of riches—Exxon, Shell, *and* Sheetz? Yes, please. We were low on gas and starving. But we had taken the promised land exit only to be met with rolling hills. Mile after mile, there was nothing. As the blocks and trees rolled by, all was silent except for a book on tape coming from the speakers.

Oliver's audiobook addiction has given him an idiosyncratic vocabulary rich in Britishisms. "My baseball hat is eluding me," he will say. "A spot of juice would do nicely!" The other day at a sleepover Oliver said, "Pancakes? What a rollicking good breakfast!" This prompted his friend's father to ask me when I picked him up, "Do you have a nineteenth-century British nanny?"

I knew the audiobook era had affected me and

Neal when we had this conversation while I made dinner:

"That school is not safe," I said. "That one girl almost died and then that boy this year did die, and the headmaster never got fired? There are only, like, two good teachers and the rest are idiots."

"Yeah," Neal said, "but where else would we send Oliver if not Hogwarts? *Durmstrang?*"

I had bought us a break from *Harry Potter* by taking the *Red Badge of Courage* audiobook out from the library, in honor of our Civil War excursion.

"The way seemed eternal," the novel intoned psychically through the car speakers. "In the clouded haze men became panic-stricken with the thought that the regiment had lost its path, and was proceeding in a perilous direction."

"That exit app sucks," said Neal.

"I already deleted it," I said.

He continued to look grim. We were almost out of gas and in the middle of a run-down Pennsylvania landscape where the locals, evidently, had no need for gas or food or glass in their window frames.

Recently, I ran into a friend who looked exasperated. I asked him if he was okay and he started right in: " *'We can shave off seven minutes if we go this way,'* she said. I knew it was a bad idea, and I was right. We got stuck in terrible traffic. And the kid is screaming that he has to pee and then wets himself. I should have stuck to my guns. Of course, then we'd have been in traffic somewhere else and *I* would have been the asshole. You're either the asshole or the victim. I'm not sure which is worse. I just drove the whole way silently, livid, wishing I could be anywhere else."

"We crucify one another in marriage, and in marriage we learn to be crucified," says Episcopal priest Father James Krueger. "In my marriage I see clearly what a schmuck I can be, and without that mirror I'm doomed."

"Quarrels," wrote Ovid, "are the dowry which married folk bring one another."

Oliver, from the backseat: "Are we going to run out of gas?"

"Almost definitely not," I said.

Neal made a noise. It was half "Ha," half "We'll see," and 100 percent infuriating.

"What?" I asked.

"Nothing," he said.

"What?" "Nothing." How many times have we said those words; how many different things they have meant.

Boxers learn to get hit without getting mad. I want that skill—not with the getting hit part, but the ability to not take personally a hideous "Ha."

"At this cry a hysterical fear and dismay beset the troops," said the audiobook. "A soldier, who heretofore had been ambitious to make the regiment into a wise little band that would proceed calmly amid the huge-appearing difficulties, suddenly sank down and buried his face in his arms with an air of bowing to a doom."

I hadn't even wanted to go on this trip. It was Neal's idea. He had noticed the boy's enthusiasm for Civil War history and realized that Gettysburg was only a hypothetical three and a half hours away. (And I quote, "Ha!") And now here we were in the middle of nowhere. I glared at Neal as he stared straight ahead at the road. In my head, I began to mentally compose a book titled *All the Problems with You: A Definitive List.*

"For some unknowable reason—which may have to do with the sex act—your spouse brings out your worst side," the poet Sparrow says. "I've never been as awful to anyone as I have been to poor Violet. Has she been 'awful' to me? No. But she has deeply resented me, in a manner that borders on the cruel. And can I blame her? Not really. That is the fucking tragedy of marriage.

Ultimately, one is responsible. You can give one thousand—or thirteen hundred—reasons why everything is the other person's fault, you can convince yourself, and often convince your partner, but you are always wrong. All your misery is created by you—absolutely all. The absolute brutal truth of this culpability is inescapable, and excruciating. Luckily, it takes you about twelve years of marriage to realize it."

A friend of mine and her husband have a "time-out" phrase that they deploy when their arguments go to this dark place: "Pig Newtons," from the Louis C.K. skit in which he describes arguing with his young daughter and losing his temper when she insists that Fig Newtons are in fact called "Pig Newtons." "You know when you get in these fights where you're both so sure you're right and the other person is being ridiculous?" my friend says. "Sometimes you just have to say, 'Pig Newtons' and walk away."

Only in a car you can't walk away, because you are trapped side by side in a large piece of metal hurtling through space at sixty miles an hour. This is why fights in cars are some of the worst fights: you can't storm off.

Oliver and I once attended a baptism at which we found ourselves giggling at the babies' different responses to being sprinkled with water: One grimaced and tried to push the priest's hand away. Another beamed in her sparkly shoes. Another balled up his fists in fury, reminding me of the classic *Onion* op-ed written by a lobster: "Just Wait 'Til I Get These Fucking Rubber Bands Off."

In his sermon, the priest told a story about his family pet Winkie, a cat who "spent her whole life biting the hand that fed her" and whose litter-box motto was "Close Enough." When Winkie died, the priest comforted his mother on the phone, saying, "She was a good kitty." His mother replied, "No, she wasn't. She was an *awful* kitty. But she was *our* kitty, and we loved her."

With kids, we see them at their worst and keep loving them. They yell, "I hate you!" and you have to be the grown-up and say, "You're mad. I still love you."

When Oliver and I are quarreling, I still hug him goodbye when we get to the drop-off door at school. "Have a good day," I say, kissing the hood of his puffy coat. Why is it so much easier to do this with children than with adults? At our worst, why can't I just think of Neal as my sometimes-awful pet cat?

"From another a shrill of lamentation rang out filled with profane allusions to a general. Men ran hither and thither, seeking with their eyes roads of escape."

• • •

But lo! Suddenly on the horizon, a cluster of businesses. At the blessed gas station, Neal pumped while I took Oliver to the bathroom. We used the drive-through of the nearby McDonald's, and the GPS rerouted us so we only lost thirty minutes to this detour rather than the years I'd imagined.

In the audiobook, Henry Fleming picked up the flag and charged.

A couple of hours later, we pulled into Gettysburg's Visitor Center, where kindly older gentlemen in ranger outfits kept handing Oliver playing cards of Civil War generals. "I got Meade and Lee!" he said ecstatically.

We watched the Visitor Center film, in which Sam Waterston does the voice of Lincoln and Morgan Freeman explains the political context of the Civil War. From old portraits, the wide, young eyes of soldiers stare out at you while the music swells, and if you don't cry, you are a sociopath. By the end I wanted to sign up for jury duty, vote, and volunteer to be a foster parent.

Then we went into the Cyclorama. I thought that meant it was going to rotate, like a revolving restaurant, but no: we stood on a platform surrounded by what was at one time the world's largest oil painting. The light changed, and spotlights plus a voiceover told the story of the Battle of Gettysburg. By chance, we were standing in the best spot, looking straight into the bank of trees from which would stream five thousand Confederate soldiers, and then twelve thousand more, in Pickett's Charge. The Confederates would reach this copse of trees to our left, then climb over the stone wall right in front of us. It seemed impossible we would survive, but then three days passed and we were still there, and the enemy was running back into the woods.

"This is the best day of my life," Oliver said as we exited the Cyclorama. "Can we go to the gift shop?"

My cousin Jeremy and I once went on a trip through historical Massachusetts with our mothers that we called the "Ye Olde Giftee Shoppe Tour." We posed in front of every swinging wooden gift-shop sign with curlicued lettering we saw. We saw a lot of them.

At the Gettysburg gift shop, Oliver picked out a dark blue Union canteen, an Abraham Lincoln T-shirt, and a little bag of toy soldiers and plastic pieces that could be assembled into Meade's headquarters. If he'd wanted a permanent Gettysburg tattoo, I would have let him get one of those, too.

That night Oliver arrayed his toy soldiers and wonky plastic house on the restaurant table while Neal and I drank wine and ate French fries. It was as pleasurable a meal as I've ever had, despite waiting half an hour for a table next to a shrieking baby.*

"We reach out for help at odd points; we bloom at unpredictable ones," notes Frank Bruni, writing in support of long family vacations and the myth of preordained "quality time." He adds, "The surest way to see the brightest colors, or the darkest ones, is to be watching and waiting and ready for them."

The next morning, we drove the Union line and the Confederate line and climbed an observation tower that let us see Dwight Eisenhower's old house and miles of battlefield. As we were getting into the car after descending, a man standing next to his motorcycle said to Oliver, "Nice canteen."

"Thanks," said Oliver.

"All I wanted when I was your age was a Confederate hat," the man said.

"Oh, I have a Union hat and a Union jacket!" said Oliver. "But not the pants. No one has good pants."

---

*We didn't speak of it at the time, because that poor mother, but a week later Neal said three words out of nowhere: "Remember that baby?"

"The one in Gettysburg who sounded like a pterodactyl?" I said.

"Yup."

That was the whole conversation.

102

"Well, you have a great day, young man," said the Confederate.

"I will," said Oliver. "You too!"

On this patch of earth 152 years earlier, our two families would have battled to the death. Now we were smiling and wishing each other a good trip, admiring one another's souvenirs.

At the end of the second day, we pulled into the parking lot of the Gettysburg cemetery and sat quietly, listening to the last section of *The Red Badge of Courage*. "He had rid himself of the red sickness of battle," the speakers said. "The sultry nightmare was in the past . . ."

The reason we had such a terrible drive, I thought, was so we could have such a lovely trip. We could have stayed home. I'd wanted to. And we would have had a fine time. But how much better to have the infuriating low and exhilarating high. Neal made us do this; it was all his fault— and we had had one of the best times of our life.

"Are we going to get out of the car?" Oliver said after a minute of sitting there.

"Shhhh!" Neal and I said at once.

From the speakers: "He turned now with a lover's thirst to images of tranquil skies, fresh meadows, cool brooks—an existence of soft and eternal peace. Over the river a golden ray of sun came through the hosts of leaden rain clouds."

A bugle played from the speakers, and the book was over.

Neal turned off the car.

"Yes," he said, "now we can get out."

As we walked toward the final stop on the tour, the cemetery, Neal glowed with the setting sun. Here he was, a small-town southerner who—I realized, for the first time in our marriage—had converted for me, a Yankee so urbanized that growing up I'd thought sparrows were baby pigeons.

He had come to the North, land of his family's enemies, with almost nothing, so we could make this life together and have this magical child. So we could take road trips and eat French fries. So we could fight and make up and listen to audiobooks and go to gift shops. So we could walk through this cemetery looking at the graves of men who died to keep the country together. I stared at him in wonder as he pointed out gravestones to Oliver, the setting sun surrounding him in a halo. Never in my life have I been more in love with anyone than I was with him at that moment.

TOAST 6

Other People, Other Cities

O happy girls, discreet in joviality!
Decoy of fingers and appeal of eyes,
Summoning the soul to be sincere and
    wise,
And love not in the flesh, but in totality!
O loves forbidden, I'll go home and start
My pipe and light my fire and break my
    heart,
And read a book on sexual morality.
        —Gerald Gould, "Monogamy," 1918

E very spring, I visit Philadelphia to speak to
a friend's journalism class. It's a city I could
imagine living in, and so I take any excuse to
go there and play a version of "House"—to play
"City." I'll probably never move away from
my hometown, but sometimes it's fun to pretend
that I could live somewhere else.

The last time I lived outside of New York,
fifteen years ago, I was studying Sanskrit at
the University of Texas at Austin. Later, I tried
to relive those days by sitting in on a weekly
Advanced Sanskrit class at U. Penn. I walked
around the campus carrying my old books and

flashcards, pretending that I was a college student again, and that the ink on my faded grammar charts was still fresh.

This is where I'd eat lunch if I were really a student here, I would think. *This is where my office would be if I were a grad student.* I imagined a tree outside my window, coffee from the campus canteen, and academic meetings with the head of the Sanskrit program, who I met when I requested permission to audit the class there. We bonded when we realized we share a favorite author: Sriharsha, a profound and risqué court poet from the twelfth century. (In my literary cosmology, there is a direct line that starts with Sriharsha, detours through Shakespeare and Dawn Powell, and ends with Louis C.K. Perhaps they are the same person, reincarnated, like an urbane Dalai Lama.)

When I was studying Sanskrit as a flailing twenty-year-old, my main interests—sex and grammar—occasionally fused, as when I translated the verses of a dirty poem that nineteenth-century Sanskritists had left untranslated due to the work's being "indelicate." I tucked my smutty translations of these verses into the book and put it back on the library shelf.

Sriharsha was the dirtiest, most grammatically inventive writer I'd ever encountered. He excelled at an exquisite grammatical trick, *slesha*—basically, allegory on speed: multiple entendre. A prime example is the famous (to Sanskritists) section of Sriharsha's *Naishadiyacaritam* called "The Pancanaliya," "The Episode of the Five Nalas." In this passage, the goddess of wisdom introduces the princess Damayanti to five suitors, all of whom appear to be King Nala, the man she hopes to marry. But, in fact, four of them are gods pretending to be Nala. The goddess uses one line to describe all five suitors at once. You can't translate this verse into English without doing it five different ways.

The chair of the Sanskrit department at U. Penn wrote a beautiful book about Sriharsha, for which I have written the only Amazon review to date (five stars).

The Five Nalas story ends with the princess staring at these five regal beings, trying to discern the king, whom she wants to marry, from the four pretenders, whom she does not. Meanwhile, King Nala, surrounded by this army of doppelgängers, questions his own existence.

"Despite the fact that the real Nala is standing right in front of her among four false Nalas," the Sanskrit chairman writes, "Damayanti is having a crisis of faith and cannot recognize the true love of her life, while Nala doubts if Damayanti will ever choose him."

Perhaps now is a good time to mention that I have always been attracted to the Sanskrit chairman. Long ago, he touched my arm and I took it for a question and moved my arm casually away. If it had been a question, he took that for an answer. Still, I look forward to our lunches more than I should.

Once we bought coffee and little pieces of chocolate from a newspaper shop and sat outside and he told me he was considering proposing to his girlfriend. He'd been married before and wondered if he could be ready to try again, to return to an institution that the first time around had proved difficult, to make a choice once and for all.

I told him that my childhood best friend, Asia, now a shrink, says you need to figure out how to build sway into a marriage, the way you do into the foundation of a building. She says that just as a tall building or bridge without room to expand or contract, to move in stiff winds, falls down, so a marriage that's too rigid crumbles at the first tremor.

"That sounds like Sanskrit grammar," the Sanskrit chairman said. "There are so many rules, but built into the rules are ways to break them. Sanskrit is all about creating potentialities— the linguistic word is 'optionality.' Wittgenstein talks about the limitations of language, though honestly there's not much you can imagine but not say in Sanskrit if you truly understand the grammar."

· · ·

When my last book came out, I went on a little DIY book tour, doing events at bookstores, churches, festivals, rock clubs, journalism schools, and a bowling alley. At one reading, there were only a few people. At another, there were hundreds. People laughed at my jokes and asked me to sign their books to friends with strange names and took me out afterward for drinks, and I loved every second of it.

The trip reminded me of being a teenager, backpacking around the world on my accumulated babysitting riches and odd jobs, feeling an infinite sense of possibility. When I was eighteen, I had romances simmering on back burners everywhere—one in Ireland, one in Sardinia, one in the Midwest, one in New York. Now I had a home I loved that I knew I'd go back to, and also things to accomplish—books to sell, lectures to give—and this appealed to my Puritan work ethic.

Before I left, Neal said he hoped I would have a good time. He said I had accomplished something and should see the trip as a victory lap. He said he hoped I would be able to fend off any advances men made on me, and that he'd be mad if I "caught feelings" for someone else. But he also said that mainly I should have fun.

And so I did.

In Houston, I saw an ex-boyfriend for a long

talk at a diner. He assuaged my enduring guilt over how I'd been a lousy girlfriend seventeen years earlier. We remembered what good friends we'd been and should be again.

In St. Louis, I spoke to the parishioners of a rector I'd written about who had died before the book came out. I saw the tiles behind which his and his wife's ashes were stored, and someone said to me, "People in this congregation will never forget this, you being here today."

In Austin, I went out drinking with some old friends. When I was hugging one of them good night by our cars, there was a sudden electricity. It took a little while for either of us to let go. "I should get back to my hotel," I said, finally, and then did. The next morning, I woke up hungover and happy.

In Miami, a scandalous friend of mine suggested that we "double-team" a surprisingly muscular journalist we met at a party. I demurred. We settled for eating tater tots on a bench outside a fast-food restaurant by the hotel.

I was the poster child for optionality. I could have all the freedom in the world, and look how well I managed it. But my friends in AA quote a line about why you shouldn't go to bars if you want to stay sober: "If you hang out in barbershops, eventually you'll get a haircut."

One night at dinner after a reading, I showed a friend of mine a photo of a colleague I planned to see on another stop of the tour. Wry and roguish, he resembled something a 3-D printer would produce after scanning head shots of my favorite actors.

"Wow," she said, looking at my phone. "Trouble."

When I was a little girl, I heard the word "soul" and asked where mine was. "Around here somewhere," my father told me, pointing at the center of my body. This image stuck in my head: the soul was invisible but present, like dark matter. It took up residence in the middle of your body, like a ghost in an old house. Today, that space just below my rib cage is where I feel lust.

I met up with this man in his town. Driving toward him, I felt a fluttering of anticipation. Butterflies are too delicate an image. The feeling of inconvenient, insistent desire was more like bats flying out from under a bridge—a black mass of beating wings.

The whole time we were sitting at the bar where we'd met up, I kept glancing at the place where his arms met his T-shirt. The impulse to touch him was barely controllable. I knew I should shake off the feeling, but I indulged it by staring, like a child impatiently waiting on line at an ice cream truck.

As I went to leave, our hands touched on the

table. Soon after, in the amber parking-lot light of a strange city, we hugged good-bye.

"You're pretty," he said into my hair.*

The attention made me feel drunk, and prettier. It's like how performer friends of mine carry themselves with greater physical self-assurance than other people, even offstage. The crowds' desire gets inside them somehow, feeds a cycle of desirability, makes them feel desirable in proportion to how much they are desired.

The bats flapped violently. I wanted to pull this man into the backseat of my car. Instead, I said good night and drove back to my hotel alone, vibrating with energy. Once back in my room, full of adrenaline, I turned on the TV and stared at it for a full hour without registering anything. I felt guilty, and elated, and I hoped I would see him again.

The next night, I did see him again, this time with other people in a public place. But then,

* "She talks like she's pretty," a friend of mine once said about another woman we know—a vicious thing to say, but the woman really did talk that way. For women, admitting that you might have any kind of attractive power constitutes bad manners. This makes it tricky to write about sex without sounding like you're saying, "Look, someone wants to sleep with me!" I realize this presents you with an obligation to scrutinize my author photo.

Oh good, you're back.

suddenly—and how naturally this seems to happen when you want it to—we were alone again, standing by our cars.

"Will you come over?" he said. "If you do, I promise I won't try to make out with you too much."

Wow, that's a good line, I thought. *He probably uses it all the time.* But it still felt tailor-made for me, for that night.

"That's not such a good idea," said my brain. "You should just go back to the hotel and go to bed early."

My body vehemently disagreed. The body is a rhetorical genius and a logistical magician—able to conjure dark corners and empty rooms, able to make insane plans seem reasonable, to make long treks effortless. That's why my favorite euphemism for affairs is "hiking the Appalachian Trail," because South Carolina governor Mark Sanford's staff said that's where he was when in fact he was in Argentina with a woman who wasn't his wife.

"Just stop thinking," my body said. "Tomorrow you can come back, the way people in Tornado Alley do after a storm. You can have all the other days forever. But for now, *shhhhh . . .*"

And because in that moment I failed to talk myself out of it, I went.

"The word is *rasa*," the chairman once told me when we were discussing the translation of a particular Sanskrit poem. "It gets translated as spirit or life force, but what it really means is wetness—sexual wetness."

In the troublesome man's apartment, I touched his arm. And then we were kissing. He pressed me into the couch with the weight of his strong, unfamiliar body. Then we chatted about music, and books, and people we knew in common, as if we were associates having an innocent nightcap, as if what we were toying with, adultery, wasn't against the law in twenty-one states. And then we were kissing again. And then it was late.

"It's time for me to go," I said.

We'd made out, but not too much—unless you think that anything when you're married to someone else is too much, in which case it was definitely way too much.

"Don't go," he said.

I wanted to stop thinking completely. My brain still had some influence, though.

"I need to go," I said.

"Just stay a little longer," he said.

I began to think the line I was drawing was academic, that maybe it wouldn't be the end of the world if I slept with this man. I hadn't had sex with anyone but my husband in fifteen years. That's a long time. If ever there were a moment to cave, this was probably it: someone I knew, but not too well; someone I liked, but didn't love. My body encouraged this train of thought.

But then my brain started flashing through potential consequences—hurting Neal, getting pregnant, falling for this man . . .

I stood up.

"You could sleep here," he said. "My bed is really comfortable. We could just sleep."

I was so tired, and he was so cute, but I made my way to the door and drove back to my hotel through the late-night chill, feeling alternately giddy and horrible.

Early the next morning, I left town. On the road, I received a text from him saying he wished we'd had more time together.

"I have a little crush on you," he said.

"Last night you said big crush," I wrote back, delaying the inevitable conversation in which I'd have to say I probably shouldn't see him again.

"Ha, okay," he replied, "big crush."

"My food!" a friend's toddler said the other day, pointing to my nine-year-old son's plate. My son was horrified. "Uh, no, that's *my* food," he said, appalled that this kid couldn't understand something so basic as what belongs to whom. *"That,"* he said, pointing to the baby's plate, "is *your* food."

So simple, right? I don't belong to this man in this other town. My husband is my husband, and other men are not. Monogamy: it's what we promise in pretty much every religious or secular marriage: "I bind you to me and loose you from all others." But like Damayanti, sometimes I look at other men and I get a little muddled. Lust creates meaning where there isn't any, builds mountains of *slesha*, turns us into children who can't tell *mine* and *not-mine* apart.

When I was a teenage babysitter, one of my charges called all women not his mother "Ada." I was flattered, though I think having an easy-to-pronounce name was a lot of it, and also it was baby-brain logic: I was called Ada, and I was a woman, and not his mother; therefore, all women not his mother were Adas. It was a category error. And now here I was making such a basic mistake when it came to the strictly limited category of men it's okay for me to kiss.

I think of all the men I've liked over the years, a new crush pretty much every month when I was single, and now every few years I've been married, and how each time I've thought, *How novel! This is delightful and new!*

When really it's the same, over and over again. I look at old diaries and I see a pattern going back to sixth grade: attraction comes on like a flu. Then, eventually, the fever breaks. I try to remember that inevitable dissolution when in the thrall of desire, but it's difficult—like, when you are sick, believing you will be well again, or trying, in the depths of slushy February, to remember the blazing sun of August. On second

116

thought, rather than illness or the weather, maybe lust is more like hunger: even if you eat the best meal you've ever had, a few hours later you're hungry again.

"Happily married women stray more often than unhappy ones," a friend told me. "It's because they don't have enough to fret about at home. Their brain needs the extra stimulation and anxiety fodder, the distraction of *Will he write me back?*"

Something about what she said sounded right. For me, wanting other people isn't about filling a deficit, the way it's said affairs usually are. It's about greed: having everything and wanting more.

"We can do whatever you want," the man on tour had said to me, like some kind of sexual genie. As if I had an erotic grocery list in my pocket waiting for just such an opportunity. (In fact, my desires are pedestrian. When I listen to music, too, I prefer greatest hits to deep cuts.)

Some people think that not getting what you want at home should serve as license to go elsewhere. To me, that seems mercenary. I imagine people placing orders at a busy deli counter: "My husband doesn't like S&M, so I would like some light bondage." "My wife doesn't kiss me passionately, so I'll need twenty minutes of necking."

One man I know has had a few one-night stands because his wife is no longer interested in sex, and she has essentially given him permission to go elsewhere for that, the way I encourage Neal to go out dancing with other people because I'm a bad dancer.

A couple of bisexual women I know have permission from their husbands, tacit or otherwise, to sleep with other women. (I am persuaded by the Kinsey scale that most of us are at one end or the other of the straight-to-gay continuum but plenty are in the middle.)

It's not like that for me, trying to get something I don't have at home. Neal denies me nothing. He is great in bed and would just as soon we had sex every day. ("Write that I have a nice penis," he says. He has a magnificent penis.) So what was I doing on that other man's couch?

I think that these things, at least for me, are not about wanting more or different or better sex; it's about wanting *other people*. And also, perhaps, it's about wanting to shake everything up. The discombobulating excitement and jealousy when someone else enters the picture throws everything into a heightened state not unlike the sexual thrall Neal and I were in when we first met. In the halo of an extramarital crush, the sex we have with each other is more intense.

But this is not all about stoking the home

fires. Some of it is about my own desire. When I saw that other man in that other town, I got to pretend that I could still be free, even though I belong to my husband until I die or he does. My interest in other men isn't about trying to trade Neal in. It's about simultaneously experiencing something new—and who do we have *here?*—and something old—my younger, freer, less responsibility-bound self.

Letting myself lust after other men means indulging in a willful delusion. I never went in for hallucinogens, but maybe that's what I want here: a psychic vacation, one in which I'm a liberated version of my normal married self.

And yet the drug isn't quite strong enough to fully take me out of this particular world. I never have been able to forget that I'm married. Even midway through a sexy dream about someone else, I will think, *What are you doing? You're married!* A sense of transgression amplifies pleasure—*I am so BAD!*—but also limits it. Ever since we met, back in the year 2000, Neal has never not been in my head. *Can't I even be free when I'm asleep?* I ask my brain. My brain says no.

In my twenties, I realized that I couldn't be a Sanskrit translator and also do the other things I wanted to do in life. As a cub reporter at the *Austin Chronicle*, I was able to attend boxing matches in rural Texas, stay out late at rock shows, and interview interesting people who passed through town. So I chose journalism over linguistics.

Some of the drama in the Five Nalas story comes not, I think, from the danger that the princess will choose wrong but from the fact that she has to choose at all. Even if your choice is perfect, you will have to put all your faith in one person, and someone will put all their faith in you. That's a lot of pressure. There's something so much easier about sitting in limbo, like the Sanskrit chairman deciding whether or not to get married.

Even after you've already chosen—maybe especially then—the choice can be terrifying. I chose well. But I dream that I might be able to pretend I'm still looking up and down a line of suitors, wondering which one to take home. I dream that I could play "Husband" like I play "City."

Driving through the Midwest after kissing the man who wasn't my husband, I looked at the cornfields and the pastures and the play-set barns and silos, with the radio on scan until it picked up Taylor Swift. (I like to leave rental-car radios on scan until I hear a song I know. It drives other people crazy, so I can do it only when I'm alone.)

So many farms and trees and thoughts about

the oddness of having someone else touch me, the thrill and the horror. How lucky I am that so far in life, lust generally has led to adventure and not tragedy. Once, twenty years ago, in bed with someone I didn't know well, I thought, *Well, this wasn't a very good idea.* But even then, the idea had been mine.

"I made out with someone," I told Neal when I got home and he asked me for the tenth time why I was acting weird. I'd spent a full hour thinking I could get away with not mentioning it, before remembering that I am terrible at keeping secrets.

"Oh yeah?" he asked.

"Yeah. It was a fling. I didn't have sex with him. I really hope you're not upset." My heart was racing. I waited to hear what he would say.

"I'm not *too* upset," he said, finally.

And when he didn't ask for details, I felt like a governor had called to stay my execution. And then we had some of the best sex of our lives. I had acclimated a little to the other man's body, even though I'd been near it for only one evening, and so Neal's body felt surprising and familiar at the same time, like getting back into a hot tub after a cold plunge.

Later, Neal had a confession, too: the night I'd been doing what I did, someone we know had told him he was attractive and he'd said she was, too. Nothing more had happened. He was proud that a pretty woman had praised him. But I heard the subtext: they wanted each other. *He has that bats-flying-out-from-under-the-bridge feeling too!* I realized, horrified.

He had joked about how we were "going on a break" while I was on tour. Now it seemed like he'd (a little bit) meant it. And I was faced with a distressing realization: he wants other people, has the same feelings of loneliness and of longing that I do. We are both Nala and Damayanti—hoping to be chosen, hoping to choose right. How do you look out into the world, see your spouse standing next to all these other people, know they're all there for you, and never choose wrong?

When Neal told me about his exchange with this woman, who exudes a cheerful sexuality I find insufferable, I was furious. Then I was upset with myself. By doing what I'd done, I'd abandoned the right to be offended. "No affair could ever be as hot as having the moral high ground," my friend Jason had once told me, and while I'd found that funny at the time, now I saw that Jason was entirely correct.

I struggled to quash my jealousy. I tried to be inspired by Neal's example. He didn't appear to be too upset by what I'd done. There was even a payoff to that "break," or whatever it was: a sexual charge that lingered for weeks. Wanting each other that powerfully after so many years is a gift. But that doesn't mean there wasn't negative fallout, too.

"Have you heard the Taylor Swift song 'Wildest Dreams'?" I asked Neal weeks later. "It was in constant rotation with 'Hotline Bling' when I was driving around on tour." On my laptop, I called up the video for "Wildest Dreams," with the old-time movie set and the giraffe. I love Taylor Swift, especially when she sexily talks about her clothes and makeup—a nice dress, red lips and rosy cheeks, a tight little skirt.

Neal got quiet. He looked pained. "Well, I can see why you'd like that song," he said. "It's about a star-crossed affair."

"Nooooo!" I said. "That didn't even occur to me! It's just a song! It was on the radio every two minutes, that's all! It wasn't like that with that guy!"

"Huh," he said. "Well, anyway, 'Blank Space' is better."

Chris Kraus's cult classic *I Love Dick* is a strange, self-indulgent, mesmerizing art project of a book in which Kraus and her husband stoked a crush she had on their friend named Dick via letter after obsessive letter. It was fun for them, and hot, until Kraus started to develop strong real-life feelings for Dick. No longer was it something the couple was playing at together; it became more than a game for her. After Dick rejected her (pointing out, rightly, that she barely knew him), she was heartbroken and unable to fully return to her husband, Sylvère Lotringer. When Lotringer was asked, years later, what the project taught him, he said, "I learned that you have to pay for indulgence."

Neal felt threatened by what I had done, and at the same time, he felt that his own flirtation was no big deal. To him, the mild intrigue with that woman was merely a validation of his virility, but to me, it felt monstrous. I hated the idea that this trollop was walking around knowing that my husband found her attractive, that he'd given her that right. This, even though if you'd asked me whether I knew he found other women attractive or whether this particular woman was objectively attractive, I would have said, "Of course."

How terribly hard it is to accept that other people feel what we feel. When politicians cheat, we say they are morally bankrupt. *Throw the bastards out.* When celebrity men lust after nannies, we shame them on tabloid covers. But when one day at work our eyes meet someone else's, it feels different. Why do we treat out-of-bounds desire as beyond our control when it happens to us but as an easily avoided abomination when it happens to others? And why do these things feel so different to us in the moment than they do to our spouses later?

For weeks, Neal and I talked and talked and talked. At some point, I became conscious of the fact that every minute of making out with that man had been paid for in hours of processing at home.

Monogamy wasn't made marital law on a whim. When we come across a fence in the middle of the road, G. K. Chesterton noted, it's probably there for a reason: "The gate or fence did not grow there. It was not set up by somnambulists who built it in their sleep. It is highly improbable that it was put there by escaped lunatics who were for some reason loose in the street. Some person had some reason for thinking it would be a good thing for somebody."

"The hardest lesson in a marriage," says my friend Asia, "is understanding the truth of the other person, believing in your heart that they are as real as you are, and their feelings matter as much. We all think that when something is wrong it will feel wrong to us, but that's the biggest lie. So many things that your partner will see as betrayal will feel to you like nothing. One of the biggest challenges of marriage is to acknowledge that your own feelings aren't the end of the story. We have to hold so many realities at once: here's me, here's you, here's us, here's the rest of the world."

"Yes, your friend is exactly right," says therapist Dr. Kelly Roberts. "The research across all of social science confirms this. And not just in marriage. When you look at doctors and patients, for example: the doctor thinks the doctor did a great job; the patient says the doctor didn't hear them. There's this gap that needs to be bridged. In a marriage, you're having that experience daily. When does the bridge ever happen? It's kind of rare. I'm sad about that. I believe, like your friend, that the more you can reflect and reach out and somehow touch what you think this person is saying or validate it, that's where that magic happens. That's where they believe that they are loved."

In all our relationships—with our parents, our children, our bosses, our clients, our landlords, our waiters—we just want to be seen. And we forget, sometimes, that other people crave that, too.

Dr. Roberts works on this in her own marriage: "I've been married thirty years. I hate golf and the sports my husband watches. And I force myself to sit on the cart with him twice a year. There's a softening in the first few minutes—

watching his joy makes me understand his humanity. I've entered his world. That's a big deal."

"Do you want to come into my world?" Oliver and his friends ask each other when they're playing Minecraft. "Yes," they say. "I am coming into your world." I wonder if in twenty years, when they are likely to be thinking about marriage, this screen time will make interpersonal empathy easier for them, because they know what it's like to create a universe and to invite someone they care about to spend time there.

A couple of weeks after the first round of processing with Neal, I found myself in Seattle, driving to a bookstore reading, feeling confident: I located the rental car's back windshield wiper on the first try. I was effortlessly navigating a city I barely knew. I'd gotten enough sleep. I'd had the exact right amount of coffee.

Then, when I was stopped at a light, a man in a suit crossing the street pointed to my car and opened and closed his hand. Unlike all the other rental cars I'd had that month, this one lacked running lights. I'd been driving through the rain for an hour with my headlights off, navigating an invisible car through a dark city, imagining I was visible and secure and safe. If I'd been oblivious to my danger there, what other hazards wasn't I noticing? Had I put my marriage at risk with what I'd done? And, *wait a second,* I was on tour again. Was Neal still in touch with that hussy?

Nala and Damayanti, they can't see each other for all the other people. They are terrified that they will lose each other in the crowd.

That Taylor Swift song "Wildest Dreams" is about wanting to be remembered. I didn't think I wanted that. But after I got home from Seattle, sitting on a bench at the Brooklyn playground where I've spent so much of the past several years, buying ices and pushing swings and breaking up kids' fights, I found myself wondering what that man was doing. When we'd hung out, he'd complimented me so many times, it was like he'd been trying to meet a quota. ("I like your bag and your glasses," he'd said as I was leaving.) What had he been thinking all those weeks since?

On my phone, I started to write him an e-mail. Then the little kids next to me climbed onto the water fountain and began to jump off like they could fly. I deleted the draft and saved the children.

"Hi," I began again later that day. Then I got a call and abandoned the e-mail.

The next day, having arrived early to pick up

my son from school, I took out my phone to try again, but another parent started talking to me, so I put my phone away.

I was reminded of one of Erma Bombeck's subtitles: *Too Tired for an Affair*.

Finally, I decided not to write; there'd be nothing to say except what that damn song said: *Remember hanging out with me? Yeah, me too.*

And then, after a few days, like a cold, the wanting to ask him went away.

At which point, as if on cue, I received a long, charming message from him. He forwarded me an e-mail he knew would make me laugh. He asked for advice. He said again that he wished we'd had more time together, and that he'd be in town in a couple of months and hoped we could meet up.

I wrote back. Something friendly but short. No flirting. *Collegial.* That seemed okay. But later, when I thought of Neal's being in touch in a similar way with that dreadful girl, it seemed not okay at all.

Sriharsha lived nine hundred years ago—nearly a *millennium*. Human beings have changed so little. When we marry, we still find ourselves looking down rows of appealing people, having to choose the same one, year after year. I've begun to suspect that fidelity is less a problem you solve than a chronic condition you manage with willpower and strategy—a decision to skip drinks, to tell the body no, or not again, or definitely only twice more. (The comedian Rick Shapiro once described a disastrous bender that led him to a crystal-clear conclusion: "Man, I really need to give up cocaine in five years.")

The notion of "good character" has fallen out of fashion. Joan Didion wrote that "one tends to think of it only in connection with homely children and United States senators who have been defeated, preferably in the primary, for reelection." But I think that staying away from other men may require cultivation of just that ideal.

Years ago, I was able to quit smoking using *Alan Carr's Easy Way to Stop Smoking*, which brainwashes you into believing that the gift you're giving yourself is not-smoking, that you're engaging not in self-denial but in a positive choice. This might be the challenge of staying faithful: seeing it not as denying yourself something but as giving yourself the experience—the security, the comfort, the pleasure—of not-cheating.

When I was in college, I had a professor who often talked about his young child. His toddler would scream in stores, "I want it!" The man told us he responded, "Good! Want it!" I remember nothing else from that class—except that the professor wore a *Star Wars* T-shirt, and that when he encouraged us to pick a performance to deconstruct, half the class went to strip clubs—but that line "Good! Want it!" has stayed with me ever since.

It reminds me of the saying "Feelings aren't facts." Sometimes we can thank our feelings for sharing and ignore them. Maybe wanting doesn't have to perfectly coincide with getting. Maybe sometimes not-getting has a value of its own. "To crave and to have are as like as a thing and its shadow," wrote Marilynne Robinson in *Housekeeping*. "For when does a berry break upon the tongue as sweetly as when one longs to taste it, and when is the taste refracted into so many hues and savors of ripeness and earth, and when do our senses know any thing so utterly as when we lack it?"

The other night, Neal and I went to a movie and then dinner. On the way home, he said, "I've been thinking about this whole other-people thing. And I think after all this time I have a new thought about it: it's a *terrible idea*. I mean, I guess I have three distinct thoughts, all totally true. One: It's hot. Two: It makes me jealous. Three: It's a terrible idea. Probably, at least until we're old, it will keep coming up, and we'll keep figuring it out, but I wanted you to know that

131

I've arrived at a new baseline feeling: *Terrible. Terrible. Terrible.*"

"Well, that's probably true," I said. "I mean, what's the best-case scenario? You flirt with someone, say, then it's like, *Well, that was fun, which means I probably shouldn't see this person again or it might become a thing I have to fight to break off, with the hurt feelings and the drama.* Or you have a lame time, and then it's like, *Wow, I went through all the taboo breaking and wrestling with my morality for* that?"

I laughed at our sudden, stupidly basic conclusions. How many conversations had we had on this subject? And what had it come down to? Infidelity: not the best idea. Stop the presses.

"You shouldn't sleep with other people when you're married," a friend once told me, "but you and your spouse can *talk* about sleeping with other people when you're in bed with each other, and that's even better."

Another friend said something similar: "You and Neal both have good imaginations. Do you know how many people I have sex with in my head? Men! Women! Whole football and cheerleading teams! Why have you been playing with fire when you could have just kept it as a fantasy?"

"Because we're sort of dumb?" I said.

"You're not dumb," another friend countered.

"Sex isn't logical, for one thing. And for another, part of what makes a fantasy hot is the idea that it could really happen."

When that man came to town, I made sure I was away. It wasn't that I didn't want to see him; I did. But I also felt like no good could come of it. Sating certain desires forestalls other pleasures. If I indulged my desire to eat ice cream for breakfast every morning, I would no longer have the pleasure of fitting into my jeans. In this case, I wanted Neal to feel secure more than I wanted to sit at a café with that man wondering if he would hold my hand.

Just once I would like to hear someone say this in their marriage vows: *How much do I love you? I love you so much that I will pass on having coffee with someone handsome and fun who I know wants me. I love you so much that even if you sort of gave me permission I wouldn't have sex with someone else because I know deep down it would bother you. I love you so much I will never be able to listen to that Taylor Swift song again without feeling sad because you thought it reminded me of another man.*

When we choose someone to marry, part of what we promise is that we will not forget that at some point, in the glow of a parking lot far from home, someone else is sure to look like a god or goddess. Maybe I need to remember that when it comes to monogamy, opening the door a crack makes it hard to keep the wind from blowing it all the way ajar, letting in more bad metaphors about doors and windows. Maybe I need to remember that I would be miserable living in Philadelphia.

Ultimately, Damayanti was able to pluck Nala from the row of gods. How?

I couldn't remember, so I texted the Sanskrit chairman.

"She doesn't really recognize the king," he wrote back, "but she recognizes the gods are not the king. There are various markers of gods: They don't blink. They float about six inches off the ground, which means there is no dust on their feet. Their garlands never wilt. And they never sweat."

Nala is a human being, which means he has things the gods don't: dust, sweat, wilting— imperfections. Other men—the heartthrob on tour, the Sanskrit chairman—they are so perfect, superhuman, gods of adventure and attention. They are too perfect. They aren't standing on the ground but floating just a few inches above it. The second I chose one, I would drag him down into the dust. He would sweat, and his garlands would wilt.

Modern relationship sage Tyler Perry says that when we're married, we need to keep in mind the 80/20 rule. Our partner, he says, will give us 80 percent of what we want. When we look at other people, we see only that they have the other 20 percent. Of course, if we ever left our partner for that other person, we would again get only 80 percent of what we want, just a different 80 percent—new joys, new problems. And looking around, we would still see the missing 20 percent in other people.

I wouldn't want to trade in my current problems for new ones with someone else.

And yet, sometimes other people are so *great.* Wouldn't it be wonderful if we *could* have our 80 percent at home and then a few 20 percents scattered about elsewhere—and by "we," I mean me and not Neal?

"There's that saying, 'You can't have your cake and eat it, too,'" says a friend of mine who, when I met her, was in a three-way relationship with her husband and another man. "But I hate that expression. Shouldn't it be 'You can't eat your cake and then still have it?' In France it's 'You can't have the butter and also the money to buy the butter.' That's better. But also, if you could find some way to have both things, shouldn't people say, 'Well done!' rather than judging you?"

I don't think her wanting more than 80 percent

135

was necessarily the cause, but I ran into her recently and she told me that she and her husband had separated.

The romantic fairy tales we grew up with—where marriage is the happy ending rather than the opening scene—are not useful for grown-ups. We have to keep living after the credits roll, navigating our way through broken appliances and aging parents and temptation-filled business trips.

But where the Brothers Grimm are useless, Sriharsha offers some comfort. Nala and Damayanti eventually marry. They encounter good luck and bad luck, jealousy and redemption. At one point, he is turned into a troll. She almost runs off with someone else. They come back together. Their marriage is full of tragedy and chaos and mystery and triumph, and it lasts until death. It's one of the great love stories of all time.

TOAST 7

"Love Is Strong as Death"

No long-term marriage is made easily, and there have been times when I've been so angry or so hurt that I thought my love would never recover. And then, in the midst of near despair, something has happened beneath the surface.

—Madeleine L'Engle,
The Irrational Season, 1977

Since Gettysburg, Oliver has cycled through a number of obsessions. One of his leading interests has been World War II, enhanced by the knowledge that two of his great-grandfathers were soldiers (one fought in the Battle of the Bulge and earned a bronze star, and another fought at Guadalcanal and earned a bronze star and a purple heart). His other fixation is Pokémon, because what child doesn't love to baffle and defeat his parents? ("Has an adult ever won a Pokémon battle?" I asked. "Not with that attitude," said a friend.)

Recently, he became fascinated by the *Titanic*. One afternoon we watched the sadder-than-we'd-recalled *A Night to Remember*. "That wasn't the best idea we *ever* had," Neal said, as we took a tear-stained Oliver to the playground, which we hoped would distract him from the tragedy of noble passengers giving up their seats and perishing in the ocean.

Luckily, Oliver ran into a friend, and they took turns riding Oliver's bike through puddles in the twilight shadow of the defunct Domino Sugar factory. It was what they call the violet hour, but that playground glowed something beyond; it looked like it was made of gold. It began misting, but we didn't make them stop playing. We had another hour until it was time to think about dinner. And they were laughing and the rolled-up cuffs of their size 10 pants were soaking up rain from puddles. There are moments in my life that from the outside looked like nothing but that I will never forget until I die, and that is one of them.

A man I know who just celebrated his thirty-ninth wedding anniversary tells me that he thinks one gift of a long marriage is a new kind of quiet:

> A number of years ago, Gerry and I were coming home from the opera and were waiting for a crosstown bus. As is her wont when we walk down the street together, we either hold hands or, more commonly, she has her arm looped through mine.

As we waited in the bus shelter with a fair number of people, there was a drunk who, upon seeing Gerry's arm wrapped in mine, pointed at us and said, "You two have been together a long time! What's your secret?" I turned to him and said in a loud voice so everyone could hear, "We don't talk to each other!" Needless to say, everyone cracked up. But later I decided that it's true: marriage is not only the talking to each other, but also the silences, which are also expressive. After people are together for a long enough time, it is perhaps the silent communication that becomes more meaningful and also more cherished. That's something that I don't think not-married people or newlyweds can understand.

"Marriage is built upon grace," writes the Christian writer Edward S. Gleason. "It is not a contract that depends upon the exchange of goods and services, based upon what each does to and for the other. Marriage is a condition of being, not doing. Marriage is based on who we are with one another. Marriage lives and grows with grace, and without grace marriage dies."

Virginia Woolf called these instances of grace "moments of great intensity," Thomas Hardy "moments of vision." Woolf says the dailiness of life is oppressive, but that every so often—on the fifth day of the week, she suggests—"a bead of sensation (between husband and wife) forms which is all the fuller and more sensitive because of the automatic customary unconscious days on either side. . . . How can a relationship endure for any length of time except under these conditions?"

Widows and widowers often say that what they remember with the most emotion aren't the big moments but the little eccentricities, as cherished in retrospect as they were annoying in life. Robin Williams's character in *Good Will Hunting* missed his wife's tendency toward flatulence in her sleep. In *About Alice*, Calvin Trillin recalls that his elegant late wife "might respond to encountering a deer on a forest path by saying, 'Wowsers!'"

"Squeezlefleeps! Flernst!" Neal says, calling our son to dinner. "Wash your hands! Shuntz! Garf! Strezel! It's *deeeener* time!"

If you'd asked me when I got married if I would ever tolerate insane accents and made-up words in my home, I would have said no. I do resist sometimes. I was livid when Neal used "Squeezlephleeps" in a game of Hangman, because Squeezlefleeps is totally spelled with an *f*. But mostly I've succumbed.

Recently I was working on a story about a

140

child welfare reform referred to as "baby courts." At dinner, I mentioned how that day I'd had to witness the struggles of families plagued with chaos and addiction and suffering.

"Did you say this reform is called 'baby courts'?" Neal said.

"Yes," I said.

He was quiet for a minute and then in a high-pitched baby voice he screamed, "I'm out of order? You're out of order! The whole damn system's out of order!"

Oliver laughed so hard he fell out of his chair.

How might we learn to appreciate our spouse's quirks in the moment? How might we teach ourselves to miss the present the way we miss the past?

While our kids watched cartoons, a friend of mine told me how she does it:

> Last night I called my husband to find out where he'd put our daughter's medicine, because he usually forgets to give it to her in the morning and so I know where it will be: wherever I left it the night before. But this time, it wasn't there. He said, "Check under the couch." Apparently, it had fallen, and in the rush to get the kids out the door, he hadn't looked for

it. I felt a flood of rage. I come home from working all day and now, while making dinner for the kids, I have to go searching under the couch? I could have yelled at him. Years ago, I would have. Instead, I shook my head and got on with my evening. I think of being married as being in the Bon Jovi song "Livin' on a Prayer." Or a dodgeball game where you're together on one side and the whole world is on the other. Feeling exhausted or getting a crush on someone or being broke or having a sick kid—it's all just another ball aimed straight at your face.

What she's describing, more or less, is the lesson of the wedding ceremony staple from the Song of Solomon in which the bride says, "My beloved spake, and said unto me, Rise up, my love, my fair one, and come away." In others words, *You and me, babe, against the world.*

When Neal eats soup, his teeth touch the spoon: clack. He slurps coffee. He tends to avoid using a knife, because he never learned how to properly cut meat, so he will bring large strips of steak to his mouth and gnaw away. He eats salad with his hands. He gets water out of the fridge in the morning, and when he does he brushes past me in our tiny kitchen while I'm making myself coffee, and how hard is it to wait two minutes?

When he gets annoyed, he sometimes curses loudly, even if I'm sleeping, even though he knows once I'm awake I never fall asleep again.

He talks so much. He loves to talk—especially, it seems, when all I want is to bury myself on the couch in my laptop and headphones. I listen to him talk about the Mets game and struggle to keep looking into his eyes while behind mine I am far away, in the Internet netherworld. And then he's annoyed that I'm distracted.

"You look like a forest creature startled in a clearing," Neal said on one of these evenings. "And all you're thinking is 'Should I bolt now? How about now?'"

I try to be better. I make an effort to close my laptop and to say, "Tell me why you're so happy about the latest Mets trade."

He tries, too. He no longer tells me every detail of his day. But still our natures creep through around the edges of our good intentions.

"God, do you have to look at your phone right now?" he says, and I did not even notice that I'd reached for it while he was talking.

"I'm sorry, but I have to do something," I say.

"I know: 'Just a minute,'" he says.

I feel guilty for a second, then angry—I have to work—and then numb as I lose myself in what I wanted to do that wasn't talking about how our team still needs a solid middle reliever.

And over and over again it goes, year after year.

I could assemble an impressive binder of data points explaining why we shouldn't have lasted even this long: boredom, wanderlust, fights over money, over sex, over parenting; fundamental differences in temperament. But staying married does not benefit from who's-done-more, who's-behaved-worse lists. Once my mother, upon hearing a friend of hers rattle off a list of all the ways in which her husband had proved disappointing, said, "Marriage is one game where the second you start keeping score, you've lost."

In 1912, as the *Titanic* was sinking, a woman named Edith Corse Evans pushed her friend Caroline Brown ahead of her into a lifeboat seat. Evans drowned that night in the cold water, one of only a few first-class women not to make it out alive.

I like to think she died happy, knowing that Brown's children would see their mother return to them. A plaque at Grace Church in Manhattan says, "in the midst of life [Evans] gave herself for others . . . trusting in Him who hath made the depth of the sea a way for the ransomed to pass over. Love is strong as death."

Viktor Frankl says the mental image of his wife helped him survive in a concentration camp. "Had I known then that my wife was dead," he writes, "I think that I would still have given myself, undisturbed by that knowledge, to the contemplation of her image, and that my mental conversation with her would have been just as vivid and just as satisfying. 'Set me like a seal upon thy heart, love is as strong as death.' "

A few years ago, Neal and I were fighting—an awful fight, our worst as of press time—and I was happy to be attending a wedding alone in New Orleans and staying with an old friend who had just had a baby.

"Do you ever fantasize about your husband dying?" I said as we pushed her daughter's stroller along the sidewalks of Mid-City. "I mean, not that I would ever *kill* Neal, of course, but sometimes I imagine, just, *poof.*"

She was quiet for several seconds, long enough for the awfulness of my statement to sink in. Yes, she and I had kept each other's darkest secrets dating back to elementary school. But this might have been over the line.

"Well," she said finally, "what I usually imagine is the widow part. Everyone would feel sorry for me. They would bring me food and flowers. I'd find out who's had crushes on me. And I'd have an excuse for wearing rumpled clothes every day. Really, what's not to fantasize about?"

One evening, Oliver, inventing ever more ways to delay brushing his teeth, enlisted me in a volleyball-like game with a gallon-sized Ziploc bag he'd inflated like a balloon. We were playing to seven points, and he was already up 4–0—having, I should say, a significant playing-field advantage in that the coffee table was right behind me and so he could throw the bag behind the table to score a point pretty easily. Then on one turn he surprised me by throwing it straight. Unprepared, I caught it right in front of my face, but not before the little plastic lock on the bag had scratched my cornea, causing me to crumple in pain. "You need to make up a better story," Neal said when he got home from work and saw me with an ice pack on my eye. "There's nothing less dignified than being blinded by a plastic bag." Injuries often come in waves in our household. Soon after the bag incident, I was at the library, trying to meet a deadline, when I got a call from the school nurse. Oliver likes visiting the school nurse because he loves going home early when he can convince her that a cough or a playground scrape warrants it. So I am usually suspicious when I see that number pop up on my phone. But I stepped into the hallway to answer, and the nurse sounded more concerned than usual. She said he'd fallen on the playground playing tag with a friend and hit his head on the concrete. I asked to talk to him, and when she put him on, he could barely talk he was crying so hard.

"I'll be right there," I said, then threw my stuff into my bag and ran to the subway.

"It could be a concussion," the nurse said when I arrived.

I took him to his doctor.

She conducted a neurological exam that showed he was probably fine but that we would have to do "concussion protocols" just to be safe. That meant waking him up every three hours that night and forbidding him from going to school or doing homework for a couple of days. Oliver smiled as if she'd put him on a strict regimen of ice cream and puppies.

"What do you want to be when you grow up?" she said as she filled out the paperwork.

"An inventor," he said.

"What are you going to invent?"

"I have a lot of designs," he said. "I'd like to tell you about them, but I don't have patents yet, so . . ." Then he told her about various inventors who were robbed of their work because they were too chatty.

"Bright kid," the doctor said, handing me the forms.

There is probably a better feeling than hearing your child praised, but I doubt it can be obtained legally.

Love and death, they meet in marriage. When you die married, you get plots side by side on a quiet hill or jars side by side on a shelf. No sign anywhere about how much you fought, how often you had sex, who had affairs, whether you liked each other's in-laws, or remembered anniversaries, or lived apart for a full year, or absolutely did not agree on where to send the kids for school. The epitaph just lists the dates you were alive, and that you were married until the end.

We undergo just a few major transitions in our life—from nonexistence to existence at birth, from nonparent to parent, from existence to nonexistence at death. We don't get to pick our parents or our children. Marriage is the one transition that's completely under our control.

Some Native American ceremonies use blankets to mark these new realities; as you are covered by a blanket when you are born and when you die, so when you marry you and your spouse are covered by one.

"Ritual can be a sacred drama of our fondest aspirations: what we were, what we are, and what we hope to be—not just measured by the meagerness of our own life's experience, but inscribed in a ritual script that we inherit from the many generations that came before us," says Rabbi Lawrence A. Hoffman. He likens ritual to the raft that takes you from one side of a river—one phase of life—to the other. "Ritual provides the exclamation points for our lives, more than it does the periods. Ritual is the wrapping that makes even the most outrageous ideals believable."

One of the Old Testament readings available for Catholic weddings is from the Book of Tobit. Sarah has been married to seven men, but to each for less than a day. Every wedding night, her husband has died. Finally, though, she marries Tobiah, and that night he wakes her up and insists that they get out of bed and pray together for mercy. He asks that God "allow us to live together to a happy old age," and God does. Was that all it took to keep Sarah from being widowed again—a man finally saying out loud that he wanted her forever, and making her wake up and say it out loud, too?

Neal and I have lived in the same Brooklyn apartment for the past ten years, and nearly every day of that decade we have said hi to our neighbors down the block, an older couple. They have children, and grandchildren, and great-grandchildren. They sit out in front of their apartment in a two-person swing and talk to people walking by. We joke that when Oliver was young, he thought his name was Qué Lindo (How Cute), because that was what they said when they saw him.

Not long ago, the old man found an injured

baby pigeon while he was walking their also-very-old dog, Brownie. He brought it home and tended to it, and it grew into a happy, healthy, full-sized pigeon. Still, it didn't fly away, but stayed with the old man. It sat outside with him during the day and at night slept in the couple's bedroom; his wife, seeming rather exasperated by their new roommate, covered the floor with newspaper. They let Oliver name the pigeon. He called her Veronica.

No one seemed to fully understand the man's obsession. One afternoon when their grown son was visiting, he said, "Dad, how about we get rid of this bird?"

"How about we get rid of *you?*" the man said.

This went on for months. Then one day the couple on the swing looked upset, and by their side sat only Brownie.

"Uh-oh," I said. "Where's Veronica?"

"The neighbor's dog . . ." the old man said, tears in his eyes.

His wife held his hand, looking so sorry for her bird-besotted husband that she seemed to mourn the very creature she'd once considered a bane.

"Those dog owners will have to move," Oliver said as we walked on toward the playground. "I don't think anyone in the neighborhood will be able to forgive them."

• • •

"Love takes off the masks that we fear we cannot live without and know we cannot live within," writes James Baldwin in *The Fire Next Time*. He uses the word "love" "as a state of being, or a state of grace—not in the infantile American sense of being made happy but in the tough and universal sense of quest and daring and growth."

If Neal slurps his soup one more time, I might pick up the bowl and throw it across the room, but we remain just as married as spouses who leave love notes in each other's briefcases. Marriage has a leveling effect, just like death. On the *Titanic*, the earls went down with the stewards.

My grandmother is ninety-nine years old. She was married to my grandfather for sixty-one years, until he died. When I was visiting her recently, I asked her, during a lull in our Scrabble game, how they stayed together for so long.

"Well," she said, "back then no one thought about leaving. It just wasn't done." She knew one couple that split up. "The wife waited for the kids to be grown and then ran off. The husband is in a nursing home now, alone, and he still talks every day about his wife and wonders why she left. He was completely blindsided. Is there anything sadder than that?"

Did my grandparents, who always seemed

151

so together, ever have hard times? "Of course," Grammy said. "I'm sorry I wasn't more open. I was scared of being too close. He wanted to talk about everything. He'd even ask me questions about how I felt, and still I kept everything in." (In her defense, Norwegians aren't known for their emotional availability.)

"So what's the secret to staying together?" I asked her.

"Be nice?" she offered.

I laughed, but that may be it, the way a secret to losing weight is to eat less. Be nice. Don't leave. That's all.

My right knee has started to hurt pretty much all the time. Some days, walking down stairs makes me feel ancient.

"You're collapsing into varus," the doctor told me when I went to have it checked.

"That sounds existential," I said. "What does it mean?"

"You have bad arthritis in your knee and you're getting a little bowlegged," he said.

The second and last time I ever went skiing, in my teens, I tore an ACL. It happened on a black diamond slope when, trying to keep up with my cousin Jeremy and a friend of his, I fell. Surgery to fix my knee failed. And so as I've walked and walked through one city after another, I've worn out my knee. I wish I could take back some of those blocks so I could use them now.

"You'll need a knee replacement eventually," the doctor said, "but try to wait as long as you can, because we only do it once and the new knee only lasts twenty years, so if you did it now, you'd be in a wheelchair by sixty."

I'm getting deeper wrinkles around my eyes. With luck, I will go to seed slowly, but my halest days are behind me. Neal and I have been there for each other's appendectomies, broken bones, and various other physical indignities. We will face more of that in the years to come. When I visited him once after a surgery, I brought him an obscenely large cat balloon that made him laugh, and an electronic solitaire game that he played for hours in a fog of painkillers, not winning once. When he stood next to me while I had a C-section, he saw my eyes fill with tears like two little swimming pools when we heard Oliver cry for the first time. Neal stood up in front of both our families and said he would love me until we die, and I may end up holding him to it.

When I ask long-married couples if they've faced any major problems in their marriage, they often surprise me with long lists. One said: "We've been married over ten years and have survived job losses, losing everything in the recession, a newborn almost dying and being in the NICU, a sudden out-of-state move, a child revealing sexual abuse—nuclear effing bomb dropped there—my husband getting a rare form of leukemia, almost dying and shuttering our business because of it. All within a five-year period."

Another person: "Twenty-three years married, and a shit-ton of crises: health, finance, child gone bat-shit crazy, addiction, sexual dysfunction (his), abortion (mine), depression . . ."

Maybe along with the standard wedding presents, we should be given a bingo card, with squares for stressors both major and minor: babysitters quitting with no notice, not being able to make a rent payment, hospitalizations. Then we could see suffering as a game: "Look, honey, we got bingo diagonally—anxiety disorder, a relative in jail, unemployment, an affair—and all before our fifteenth anniversary! The Joneses took twenty years to bingo, but they did have the rare combination of teenage pregnancy and house fire. Good game, Joneses."

"To love somebody is not just a strong feeling—it is a decision, it is a judgment, it is a promise," writes psychologist Erich Fromm. "If love were only a feeling, there would be no basis for the promise to love each other forever. A feeling comes and it may go. How can I judge that it will stay forever, when my act does not involve judgment and decision?"

"When you fall in love, it doesn't feel like a choice," a friend of mine says. "It feels like fate. And so then when the passionate love cools in your marriage, it's hard to feel like that's not fate, too. It's hard to remember that letting yourself fall in love with this person and marrying them was a choice, and loving them again can be a choice, too."

A woman whose husband is in a psychiatric ward for the seventh time since they were married, twenty-one years ago, told me:

> I feel like I didn't sign up for this. I had no idea. I agree that marriage is a commitment. I'm not just staying in it because of that, because I made a promise. I'm staying in it because he's a good father and I have hope. But it sucks being a single mom. He was in the hospital for Hurricane Sandy. It's tough. My mom's not feeling so well. But I guess I do feel like I have hope and I feel like I have an obligation to him. He never asked for this.

"I just can't do it anymore," a friend said over the phone. She was furious with her husband, who she felt resented her for being chronically ill.

But he wasn't saying she was a burden, I pointed out. Couldn't she just own it until she was better? Like, "Yeah, I'm a burden! Can't do a thing about it. Please get me some water?" She would take care of him if he were sick, I pointed out.

"But, honestly, I don't know if I would have been able to," she said. "He's a better person than I am."

"Well then," I said, "there's something you can both be grateful for in the middle of all this: that you're the one who got sick, not him."

A woman who lives in a small town in the middle of the country tells me she fell hard in love with her husband the first moment she met him in a bar, and that in those early days they couldn't keep their hands off each other: "We dripped so much candle wax in our bedroom messing around that the clock next to the bed looked like a vampire's."

Three years later, they moved into a big house and quickly had two children. "My husband calls those the salad days," she says. They had good jobs, good kids, a good house. But the good times didn't last. She developed postpartum depression, and then bipolar disorder, and then had an affair: "I was at home with two toddlers, whispering into my cell phone while my boyfriend whispered right back from his basement, so his wife wouldn't hear him."

When the affair ended, she was plagued by guilt:

> I had sinned. I couldn't wash off the awful things I'd done. I had nearly destroyed my little family. I couldn't let it happen again. So I ate. I ate to stanch the guilt I felt at how disappointed my late father would have been. I ate so my husband wouldn't chase me around the house anymore asking for sex. I ate so no man would even take a second glance at me, but instead would avoid looking at a physically distorted obese woman with a pretty face. . . . And yet—he stayed. He stayed with me through the cheating, through the depression, through me mutilating my body with food, all the while threatening to leave him, as if he didn't have reason enough to leave me at any minute. He stayed, and he loved me, a broken person with a broken brain.

Last night I woke up at two a.m. and couldn't get back to sleep. I took a Tylenol PM and lay down on the couch, staring at the Halloween decorations, Oliver's backpack, the pile of papers on the table. The ceiling fan spun the dollar-store bats in wobbling arcs around the room. The fish filter hummed. In the kitchen, the coffeemaker was preset, its blue light glowing with promise.

When I was a girl, I sometimes slept with a row of pillows in bed with me, imagining the pillow-man as a real person. I fantasized about sharing a bed. I dreamed of beds in farmhouses, in apartments and in tents, in the country and in the city. I wanted company and intimacy, understanding and warmth. Now I have those things, and only sometimes do I catch glimpses of how good I have it.

When Oliver was younger and would climb into bed with us at dawn and go back to sleep for an hour until the alarm went off, I would feel fortunate and peaceful, lying there in between my husband and my son, half-asleep and half-awake, half-hoping the sun would never rise. But most days, I see only the homework undone, or the dishes unwashed, or the floors unvacuumed.

If I'd left Neal the various times I'd considered it, I'd have other things now—probably other men, other apartments, different sounds out the window. But on Tylenol PM at two in the morning, lying on the couch, watching the little bats waft in the breeze, I know this in my heart: my life with this man is the best of all possible worlds. Sometimes maybe it's the worst, too, but it's the only one that's truly all mine.

When we're born, our brains and bodies are

capable of just about anything. As we grow, our brains prune the neurons we don't need, just as our bodies reinforce the muscles we use most often. Our abilities narrow, our worlds narrow, our lives narrow, until we are a person whose life is not full of infinite potential but, instead, is teeming with memories of things done and left undone. At forty, I am slowly coming to terms with the elementary notion that being in this world means giving up on other worlds.

When I was younger, I imagined I'd have several children, but it didn't work out that way. I have one son and an adult stepson. I might be able to get pregnant now, but not without a lot of effort and a lot of explaining to do, as Neal had a vasectomy several years ago. So I'm reconciled: my genes and womb have done all they're going to do. And even if I'd had a dozen children, one day they would grow up and leave me and Neal alone with each other.

One woman tells me that her father, married for forty-eight years, gave her a lesson in the role children should play in a marriage:

> I was being a selfish teenager and it was hurting my mom and making my dad angry. He sat me down and said, "I need to remind you: you are not the reason we got married. You are a wonderful by-product. But you need to know that I

loved your mom before you were even a thought. And after you've left this house, I will still love her." I was shocked. It was like, "You are a blip on the screen of our relationship."

On board the *Titanic*, Edith Corse Evans's shipmate Ida Straus declined a lifeboat seat so that she and her husband could die together. The long-married sometimes die at the same time, either by desire or chance. A California couple married for sixty-seven years died at home, the wife within hours of her husband. In the memoir of her husband's illness, Molly Haskell writes, "I felt that if Andrew died, I would die, too. Not by suicide, but just automatically, as bees die when they are detached from the hive."

These stories are more romantic to me than *Romeo and Juliet*. When young lovers say life isn't worth living without the other, what do they know? They haven't lived life yet. When old couples say it, that means something.

Father Hartt tells me that, while of course there are plenty of happily unmarried people, some in his parish feel the lack of marriage:

There are a lot of really broken people. Unfortunately, especially for women, your sense of self and your viability is so under assault from this terrible culture focused on youth. Men have permission for eternal childhoods. So many people I know by all rights should have been married. They're sad. They're alone. They're hurt. They're angry at all the sexual passing along. Men as well as women. So let's have another reason for marriage. Even people who are divorced have a certain dignity around the fact that that had happened. We need to look at marriage from the standpoint of aging, from the standpoint of cultural disposability, and look to an institution that says, "You are precious. Your union is precious. The community is supposed to think your union is precious. We're going to do this in public so everybody knows and everybody is accountable." That's huge. It's the opposite of saying you're disposable or that there's no hope or help for you if things go awry.

Over lunch, an eighty-four-year-old man tells me how glad he is that his marriage has lasted. He and his wife hit the skids a couple of times in the 1980s. On their twenty-second anniversary, they went to a guru in upstate New York.

"We're having problems," they said.

"You should do better," said the guru.

The idea that they had a choice in the matter was a revelation. The guru was basically saying, "You have problems? Don't."

The man and his wife had major financial difficulties a few years later, but they weathered that, too, and now here they are, celebrating their fifty-eighth anniversary, living close to their four grown children and their grandchildren.

I tell him my friends are getting divorced because they've fallen out of love. He laughs. "Instead of 'I'm not in love anymore, I need to leave,'" he says, "how about: 'I don't think I'm in love anymore and I need to know why.'"

Nearly everyone I've talked to who's been married thirty, forty, fifty years has said something similar: that affection, love, lust—whether for your partner or for other people—these feelings come and go. That although the day-to-day struggles can feel impossible, the years zip by. Nearly all of them told me that they'd considered divorce at one point or another, and were glad they'd stayed.

One woman married for twenty-five years said, "Many times, it simply seemed easier to stay than to figure out how to divvy up the books. And then we broke on through to the other side . . . like playing a video game where you suddenly hit a new level that you didn't even know was there."

"When I wanted to leave, it didn't seem like a

good time for various reasons," a woman married for fifteen years told me, "and then when it *was* a convenient time, I no longer wanted to. And so you sort of stagger on and then you think, 'He makes me crazy sometimes, but what would it be like not to have him around? I wouldn't like it.' "

Another woman, who's been married to her wife for as long as we've had marriage equality, referred me to a poem called "The Longly-Weds Know," which begins:

> That it isn't about the Golden Anniversary
>   at all,
> But about all the unremarkable years
> that Hallmark doesn't even make a card
>   for.
>
> It's about the 2nd anniversary when they
>   were surprised
> to find they cared for each other more
>   than last year
>
> And the 4th when both kids had chicken-
>   pox
> and she threw her shoe at him for no real
>   reason

The other night, Neal returned home from watching a basketball game with a friend, and he looked shell-shocked. The bar owner had come over to talk with Neal and our friend and ended up telling them the story of his divorce.

"He said he had an affair and when his wife found out, she threw him out and won't let him see the kids," Neal told me. "He's spent all his money on lawyers. His credit cards are maxed out. Worst of all, his kids are babies, and he's missing months of their lives. He says it's all because he had a fling with 'some blond woman.' He kept saying that phrase, 'all because of some blond woman.' He looked like he'd been hit by a truck. Let's never get divorced."

Bored at work, I used to Google ex-boyfriends. I thought of this as like the David Carr book *The Night of the Gun*, except that where Carr went back and reported on his years of addiction, I tried to figure out where my junior high boyfriend was now. Neal nicknamed me "Decades-Later Detective."

One day, I turned up a video of the writer Brad Will, who I'd hung out with when I was eighteen. During our ensuing years as pen pals, he'd stolen a disability poster from a Colorado library—a big picture of a smiling Bill Clinton with the words "America Needs You to Keep the Promise of ADA."

Sitting at my desk in a Manhattan newsroom, I watched the video on YouTube. It showed him in Mexico, covering Oaxaca as a reporter for a

164

site called Indymedia. The camera recorded him being shot, and then bleeding, and then dead—lying on the pavement in his underwear. The finality of death hit me hard. How obvious: death is forever, and yet how shocking it seemed in that moment. All the tempters in my life, beckoning me out of marriage—they'll die, too. I don't look up exes so much these days.

Last night I had a dream that either Neal or I was dying; it wasn't quite clear in the dream haze which one. "I'm here," I was saying when I woke up.

I found myself grateful that Neal wasn't dead and I wasn't, either. When I imagine him dead, I feel myself missing him—missing even, maybe especially, the things about him that irk me, down to the clacking of his teeth on his spoon while eating cereal. I think maybe what they say is true: that you can't be loved if you're perfect; only the flawed, the King Nalas, are lovable.

I'm glad you're not dead, I thought, looking at Neal still sleeping.

Then, like most mornings, I got out of bed, turned off the night-light, and switched on the aquarium light for Oliver's pet turtle, Ginny, and her five fish roommates. The fish are nineteen-cent feeder goldfish who the turtle befriended instead of eating, making her dinner our new pets. I packed Oliver's snack, woke him up, and started making breakfast—doing the work of keeping our family going, hoping that these little actions will help us have a good day, a good week, a good life.

What does it mean to say you're present? It's defiance: Elaine Stritch singing, "I'm Still Here." It's what you say when you arrive after being somewhere else. It's reassuring. It means you've come back, or that you haven't left. And maybe eventually it means "I'm here now, so you can let go."

Thomas Jefferson sat by his wife's bedside as she lay dying. They had been through so much, losing child after child. And now, at just thirty-three, she was dying, too. They had been reading a book together, *Tristram Shandy*, and she had begun to write out a paragraph. He picked up the copying in his own, stronger handwriting: "I kiss thy hand to bid adieu, every absence which follows it, are preludes to that eternal separation which we are shortly to make!" He kept that piece of paper close for the rest of his life.

In my dream, either I was saying I wasn't dead yet or that I was staying by Neal's side as he lay dying. If we stay together, we could be that for each other. I imagine me saying, "I'm here" to him or him saying it to me. And on that day it will mean: *You're not going to die alone. Look at that. You stayed and I stayed, and here we are at the end. The other people we had crushes on—where are they now? The fights—who can remember what they were about? The money problems—do they matter? The school concerts, the bills, the nights one of us slept on the couch, the jokes, the trips, the irritable mornings, the parties, the weeks of no sex or lots of sex— they swirl into a life together. That was the race, and this is the ribbon. That was the trail, and this is the crest. Those were the bricks and mortar, and this is the house we built.*

Stirring pancake batter, I look around our little apartment. I have to make sure Oliver is getting dressed. I have to remember to pick up groceries on the way home. I have to make a million calls. None of it, right this second, matters.

"Where'd you go?" Neal mumbles from the bedroom, still half-asleep.

"Nowhere," I say. "Nowhere at all."

EPILOGUE

One Toast I Would Actually Give

There is sure to be another flood toward, and these couples are coming to the ark. Here comes a pair of very strange beasts, which in all tongues are called fools.
> —William Shakespeare,
> *As You Like It*, 1599

Exactly a year after the Minneapolis trip with the missed flights, Neal and I went to a friend's wedding in the Dominican Republic. ("Destination wedding on second marriage—bold move," another friend said.)

This friend had been married to someone else when we'd met him. Then we'd been friends through his divorce—I'd helped him assemble Ikea furniture and paint his bachelor pad. And I'd observed with prurient glee his Tinder-tastic dating life, and then celebrated when he met his cool new girlfriend, now fiancée.

Over the past nine years, his daughter and our son, just a few months apart in age, have enjoyed countless playdates. We've watched them go from putting acorns in their mouths, to learning how to ride scooters, to racing through apartments and parks and eating buttered pasta and cut-up cucumbers while we drank coffee or beer, to watching *Spy Kids 2* for the tenth time, to building Lego fortresses and asking us to please leave them alone.

In the run-up to the wedding, Neal and I were getting along better than we had in years. We were closer, and laughing more and feeling more committed. Oliver had a lot of friends; parenting now largely involved making stovetop popcorn and handing it to the kids while they traded Pokémon cards. We'd reached a new, happier normal.

And yet.

A week before our trip, Neal realized he'd misplaced his passport, prompting a weeklong search through various closets and basements within a 150-mile radius, during which I began a stressful new job. I'd had to delay my flight a few days because of this opportunity—a gig from which I was terrified of being fired because I'd already mentally used the money to pay off our debts. Oliver became sick upon touching down on foreign soil and spent two days throwing up and going in and out of a fever. With every text message, I panicked and second-guessed all of Neal's decisions and sent him directions to Dominican urgent-care clinics.

And yet again.

By Saturday, our friend's wedding day, the

three of us, all with our passports and our normal body temperatures, were sitting on gold chairs on a patio at the edge of a cliff, looking out over the Caribbean Sea while Yaz's "Only You" played from the speakers and our friend stood under an interfaith canopy and his girlfriend walked toward him, her parents flanking her on either side, and I teared up and reached over Oliver's head to put my hand on Neal's shoulder.

"What should we say in our vows?" this friend had asked me a few weeks earlier, over a diner lunch, while our kids borrowed our phones to craft stories in emoji language and dared each other to eat stupid numbers of crackers.

I tried to come up with something he could use.
Marriage isn't a happiness factory.
He knows that. He was married before.
Staying married is a decision, an active choice at once creative and brave. It can be rewarding, distressing, mystifying, enlivening, or all those things at once.
Would that suggest that he should have stayed in his first marriage? I didn't mean that.
"Saying you're going to stay together is plenty," I told him finally. "You don't have to gild the lily. 'I do' covers it."
The friend they had perform the ceremony did a lovely job. They opened up the mike for toasts, and there followed the usual cheery hodgepodge

of sentiment. While I hadn't planned on giving a toast, I did think of something I might say. But by the time I felt the impulse, that part of the night was ending and Neal was being called on to do a song-as-toast.

"I wrote this on the way here," he joked, waiting for the backing music to come on, and then he did a devastating cover of "I Would Die 4 U" by Prince, who had died days before. Everyone sang along with the chorus and hugged each other and cried.

"Your friend is so talented," the groom's father told his son. "How amazing that he wrote that song just for you."

With that, it was indisputable: Neal had officially won the wedding. He had been the good dad restoring a sick child to health and the king of rehearsal-dinner karaoke (every phone in the place, including the bartenders', came out when he took on Sisqó's "Thong Song"). He'd played Shark and Minnows with the kids and drunk beer with the guys, endearing himself to partygoers of all ages.

"Oh, how nice," he would say the morning after the wedding, showing me a list of Facebook friend requests from roughly everyone on the guest list. (I quickly checked my account to discover three invites; two were spam.)

I was reminded of an actress friend who says that seeing her husband in plays rekindles her attraction to him. When other people look at him, she is able to "reobjectify" this man who day-to-day is so familiar. Watching Neal at this wedding, I was reminded of how fortunate I am.

And so this is what I would have said in my toast:

I am so happy for you. But I'm just as happy for all of us here today. By getting married, you are doing something religious in the oldest sense of the word: bringing us together in a common spiritual purpose, making a community where there wasn't one before.

Making a relationship official and public changes it. When you have witnesses from both families, each person's tribe is on its own side, and when the couple walks back up the aisle after getting married, they're like the pull tab on a zipper, merging the two sides into one family for the rest of human history.

Today you showed, may the atheists in the room forgive me, faith—faith in each other, in all of us assembled here, and in yourself; faith that together we will be able to do something enormous: help you stay together, loving each other, until you die.

I have only two pieces of advice about marriage.

The first is that my mother is right. The way you stay married is simple: you don't get divorced. All the couples therapy and communication seminars in the world won't save you if you aren't prepared to close your eyes and hug the mainmast through a storm. One of the best skills you can cultivate in a marriage is, ironically, stubbornness.

Perhaps it helps to know that the demise of marriage as an institution has been overstated for centuries. "The estate of marriage has universally fallen into such awful disrepute," Martin Luther wrote in 1522. In 1914, another revolutionary agitator, Emma Goldman, noted, "That marriage is a failure none but the very stupid would deny." As proof she quoted the *astronomical* rate of 73 divorces for a population of 100,000.

The second is that a marriage is made up not of years of faithful service but of moments of grace. Good manners help, but the couples who endure are not always the ones who are the most compatible or the best behaved, the ones who take out the trash without being asked and never look at another person with lust and who balance their checkbook and agree on whether or not to sleep-train their kids and who "chose well."

No, the marriages that thrive are the ones between people who appreciate grace. Such grace appears in those moments when you suddenly see the person you've always known just as you've always known them but also as someone surprising, someone brand-new. Catholic weddings often include a reading from Genesis. Upon seeing Eve, Adam says, "This at last is bone of my bones and flesh of my flesh." If weddings required a catchphrase, I think that could be it: "At last."

At a wedding, the bride and groom transform into archetypes. The here and now becomes what experts in ritual describe as "a moment of eternity and eternal return." We are connected backward to those who have been joined together before us, going all the way back to prehistory, and forward, to those who will continue to find each other after we are dead.

When we marry, we are saying that our union—however messy or fraught or complicated it might also be—is holy, too. We invite those we love to consecrate it with their toasts.

"The Jewish way of appreciating life at its finest is the language of blessing," says Rabbi Lawrence A. Hoffman, calling that word akin to "grace." " 'What a blessing I found you,' you might say to your partner. 'What a blessing to sit here and hold hands, or to enjoy the sunset and look at you and know we are together.' "

Such a moment of grace is what we experience when we watch a bride walking down the aisle. Here she is, our old friend, or daughter, or cousin, or aunt. She is the person we know, but suddenly she's different, too. This person approaches the altar as if from out of the clouds, as though she's come from another world with a message for us.

And she has.

That message is: Remember this—how surprising and miraculous and startling grace feels. Especially remember it when your wife tells you you've done everything wrong or your husband loses his passport or when your attractive colleague sits next to you at a work conference or for whatever other reason you feel the urge to get on a plane and fly as far away as possible. You need something in those moments to hold on to, so you can remember why it might be better to stay. Today we've all been handed such a moment.

May you have a million more in the years to come: when you see your husband or wife through a crowd and think, "Who is *that?*" and realize it's the person you picked and who picked you five, twenty, fifty years before.

You can't plan for grace. These moments are like shooting stars: you see them only if you're watching, and you see them more clearly when it's dark.

Most of those moments will be private. No one but you will see them. Today is one that we all got to see. Thank you for that. Now when you have trouble, we can remind you of today, a day in which we saw you promise to stay, and we promised to help.

Weddings remind us why we were put on earth—to witness these moments, to let them bind us together. May we always remember this: nothing more nor less than these moments of grace will keep you— will keep us—together, all the days of our lives.

Cheers.

APPENDIX

Toward a More Realistic Reception Playlist

The usual wedding party playlist reinforces the idea of marriage as something that happens under a rom-com's closing credits. Here are a few more relevant options:

"All the Right Reasons"—The Jayhawks

"La Chanson des Vieux Amants"—Jacques Brel

Devotion and Doubt (whole album)—
Richard Buckner

"Farther Along" (gospel hymn)—Dolly Parton,
Linda Ronstadt, and Emmylou Harris

"I Really Don't Want to Know"—Elvis Presley

"In My Life"—The Beatles

"In Spite of Ourselves"—
John Prine and Iris DeMent

Lemonade (whole album)—Beyoncé

"Livin' on a Prayer"—Bon Jovi

"On the Other Hand"—Randy Travis

"Right Down the Line"—Gerry Rafferty

"Strangers"—The Kinks

"There Will Be No Divorce"—
The Mountain Goats

"Thin Line Between Love and Hate"—
The Persuaders

"2 Way Street"—Slick Rick

"We're Gonna Hold On"—
Tammy Wynette and George Jones

"Wishing Well"—Jo Dee Messina

Acknowledgments

In 2015, in a fit of pique, I wrote an essay about fighting with my husband. That piece, "The Wedding Toast I'll Never Give," was named No. 41 on the list of most-read stories in the *New York Times* that year (but who's counting). Thanks to Dan Jones, for expertly editing it for the Modern Love column, and to my terrific agent, Daniel Greenberg, for seeing it as a book (and to his colleagues Jim Levine and Tim Wojcik for their support).

Thank you, friends and strangers I interviewed, for being so frank with me. Particular gratitude goes to my oldest friend, the gifted therapist Asia Wong, and to the brilliant reporter Jason Zinoman, for their wise comments on early drafts.

Thanks to everyone who abetted my research, particularly Paul Hartt, Don Waring, Lawrence A. Hoffman, Nura Manzavi, Christian Rada, Evyatar Marienberg, Victor Hori, Martha Ertman, Naomi R. Cahn, and Kelly Roberts.

I wrote this book in the glorious New York Public Library's Allen Room—the best place in the world to work, and located conveniently across the street from my publisher.

W. W. Norton & Company is just the greatest.

I adore the whole gang, especially Meredith McGinnis, Nomi Victor, Kyle Radler, Elisabeth Kerr, Steve Colca, eternally vigilant assistants Ryan Harrington and Sarah Bolling, and enchantingly compulsive copy editor Bonnie Thompson. Most of all, thanks to my literary soul mate Tom Mayer, the kind of insightful, creative, generous editor they say doesn't exist anymore.

Thanks to my parents for their good advice. Most of all, thank you to Neal, Blake, and Oliver, for being the best things that ever happened to me.

Notes

EPIGRAPH

10 **"Marriage is a relationship far more engrossing":** Mike Mason, *The Mystery of Marriage* (Portland, OR: Multnomah Press, 1985), pp. 34–35.

INTRODUCTION: "DO YOU KNOW
WHY YOU'RE HERE?"

13 **"Like everything which is not the involuntary result":** W. H. Auden, Introduction to "Marriage," *A Certain World* (New York: Viking, 1970), p. 248.

14 **Finding something new or helpful to say about marriage:** The best-man speech Benedict Cumberbatch delivers in *Sherlock* is a pop-culture wedding toast gold standard. "The Sign of Three," season 3, episode 2, January 26, 2014.

14 **"Don't go to bed angry":** "Let not the sun go down upon your wrath," Ephesians 4:26, King James Version.

15 **the question *Do you know why you're here?* is vital to marriage:** Interview of Father Paul J. Hartt by the author, January 23, 2016.

16 **"I am not altogether sure the people**

know why they're there": Pope Francis has said something similar, going so far as to say that today's young couples, having grown up in a world where so much is disposable, don't grasp the permanence of marriage, rendering their unions "null." He added, "The crisis of marriage is because people do not know what the sacrament is, the beauty of the sacrament; they do not know that it is indissoluble, that it is for one's entire life." Cindy Wooden, "Too Many Couples Do Not Understand Marriage Is for Life, Pope Says," *National Catholic Reporter*, June 18, 2016; accessed online.

16 **"It's often tough to get couples grappling":** Interview of Father Don Waring by the author, December 7, 2015.

17 **"I'm afraid I think this rage for happiness rather vulgar":** George Bernard Shaw, *Getting Married* (1908; repr., Studio City, CA: Players Press, 1995), p. 73.

17 **"On one hand, I have a lot of compassion":** Interview of Rabbi David Adelson by the author, March 7, 2016.

18 **The main problem with marriage may be:** "Most of the complaints about the institution of holy matrimony arise not because it is worse than the rest of life, but because it is not incomparably better,"

note John Levy and Ruth Monroe. "We don't expect life to be all sunshine and roses, or even beer and skittles [an old term for bowling]. But somehow we do expect marriage to be that way." *The Happy Family* (New York: Knopf, 1945), pp. 46 and 65.

19 **"The reason that people want to get married":** Interview with Rabbi Lawrence A. Hoffman by the author, July 28, 2016.

TOAST 1: PAYING FOR
EACH OTHER'S MISTAKES

21 **"If a man could receive the advantages of marriage":** Theodor Gottlieb von Hippel, *On Marriage*, trans. Timothy F. Sellner (Detroit: Wayne State University Press, 1994), p. 83.

21 **While away at a conference in Minneapolis:** A version of this essay ran in the *New York Times* Modern Love column as "The Wedding Toast I'll Never Give," July 16, 2015.

22 **Money has served:** People tend to marry within their class, limiting economic mobility. Rich Morin, "New Academic Study Links Rising Income Inequality to 'Assortative Mating,'" Pew Research Center, January 29, 2014.

26 **"Dew is a Buddhist symbol of impermanence":** I exchanged e-mails with my old

McGill University professor Victor Hori, and he confirmed that this was a viable reading of the Issa poem. For more on Issa, he recommended the Taitetsu Unno book *River of Fire, River of Water*. He also said: "Issa had tried to start a family late in life. He married at age forty-nine or fifty. His firstborn died, and then his daughter died. . . . When Issa says, 'The world of dew is / A world of dew,' he is saying that the Buddhist picture of the world indeed is true; Buddhist philosophy is correct. But one who understands Buddhist philosophy does not necessarily transcend the pain and anguish one feels when a baby dies. 'And yet, and yet' means 'I can't help crying.' Unno says that one reader said this shows that Issa did not really understand Buddhism. But Unno himself says that a Buddha feels that emotional pain. So I think Unno would agree with you. Marriage is not all pleasant; it's a very rocky road; there is lots of venting of anger—and yet, and yet." E-mail exchange January 25–28, 2016.

27 **"You don't get divorced":** In the 2011 Martin Scorsese movie *George Harrison: Living in the Material World*, Olivia Harrison, speaking about how they stayed together in spite of his affairs, says, with a smile: "What's the secret of a long

marriage? You don't get divorced." In the background, you can hear members of the crew cackling.

27 **"We never wanted to get divorced at the same time":** British *Glamour*, June 2013.

30 **"Mary and I have been married forty-seven years":** Irving Fein, *Jack Benny: An Intimate Biography* (New York: Putnam, 1976), p. 56.

30 **"All blessings are mixed":** John Updike, *Too Far to Go: The Maples Stories* (1956; repr., New York: Fawcett, 1982). This quote appears in the foreword (written in 1979): "That a marriage ends is less than ideal; but all things end under heaven, and if temporality is held to be invalidating, then nothing real succeeds. The moral of these stories is that all blessings are mixed."

TOAST 2: THE BORING PARTS

33 **"Each of us must live with a full measure of loneliness":** Jim Harrison, *Dalva: A Novel* (1988; repr., New York: Simon & Schuster, 1989), p. 71. See also Henry Green, "Falling in Love," *Esquire*, 1955, in Matthew Yorke, ed., *Surviving: The Uncollected Writings of Henry Green* (London: Chatto & Windus, 1992), pp. 192–93. Green writes, "We are all animals, and therefore, we are continually being

attracted. That this attraction should extend to what is called love is a human misfortune cultivated by novelists. It is the horror we feel of ourselves, that is of being alone with ourselves, which draws us to love, but this love should happen only once, and never be repeated, if we have, as we should, learnt our lesson, which is that we are, all and each one of us, always and always alone."

40 **"walk through fire" or "take a bullet":** Savage says: "You know when people always say, when they talk about the people they love most in their lives, 'I would take a bullet for this person, I would walk through fire for this person'? That's hurt. You're saying, 'I would hurt for this person.' In a really profound and life-threatening way. 'I would take a bullet. I would walk through fire.' Infidelity, when people believe in monogamy and monogamy is what they want, infidelity is that bullet. . . . If you look at your partner and think, 'I love you so much I could take a bullet for you,' just if and when it happens, remember that feeling, because that's the moment where you take the bullet." Dan Savage, "An Open Letter to People Thinking About Checking to See if Their Husbands or Wives Were on Ashley Madison," *The Stranger*, August 19, 2015. He also says something similar in

"Cheating Happens," *Death, Sex, & Money* podcast, February 25, 2015.

41 **Newt Gingrich said:** James V. Grimaldi, "Marianne Gingrich, Newt's Ex-Wife, Says He Wanted 'Open Marriage,'" *Washington Post*, January 19, 2012.

41 **evidently less of an embarrassment:** Dan Savage, "Voters Prefer Newt Gingrich's Adultery to Open Marriage," *New York Times*, June 20, 2014.

41 **"I am stating that emotional entanglements":** Levy and Monroe, *The Happy Family*, p. 100.

43 **at least one in ten:** In a *Washington Post* article, the author cited Shere Hite's 1991 study saying that 70 percent of married women have cheated and a 2004 University of Chicago study saying that 72 percent of married men have had at least one affair. Eric Anderson, "Five Myths About Cheating," *Washington Post*, February 13, 2012. The psychologist and researcher Geneviève Beaulieu-Pelletier told me that the probability of reporting at least one lifetime incident of what she calls "extradyadic" sex is 19 to 34 percent among married people (per an oft-cited study Michael W. Wiederman, "Extramarital Sex: Prevalence and Correlates in a National Survey," *Journal of Sex Research* 34, no.

2 (1997): 167–74). Interview of Geneviève Beaulieu-Pelletier by the author, March 25, 2016. See also Beaulieu-Pelletier et al., "The Role of Attachment Avoidance in Extradyadic Sex," *Attachment & Human Development* 13, no. 3 (May 2011), 293–313. And: University of Montreal, "Infidelity Dissected: New Research on Why People Cheat," *ScienceDaily*, September 13, 2008.

44 **"the things that nurture love":** Interview of Esther Perel by the author, September 9, 2016. See also her book *Mating in Captivity*.

46 **the free-love Kerista Commune:** There's a record of the commune at Kerista.com. Under the headline it reads, in tiny print, "We didn't save the world. We didn't even try. We talked about it a lot." I want that on a mug. Retrieved July 10, 2016.

48 **Friends and colleagues can't take refuge:** In 1894, Edward Carpenter (called "the gay godfather of the British left") wrote, "Love is fed not by what it takes, but by what it gives, and that excellent dual love of man and wife must be fed also by the love they give to others." This quote appears in Marie Carmichael Stopes, *Married Love* (New York: Putnam, 1931), p. 120. The Book of Common Prayer has the congregation pray that the married couple find "wisdom and

devotion in the ordering of their common life," such that they may "reach out in love and concern for others."

52   **"Marriage involves more suffering than most":** Sparrow, letter to the author, June 7, 2016.

TOAST 3: CONTAINING MULTITUDES

57   **"Marriage is people":** Maurice Lamm, *The Jewish Way in Love and Marriage* (Middle Village, NY: Jonathan David Publishers, 1991), p. 117: "Marriage is people. Like sex, marriage cannot be abstracted from character. Good people make for good marriages, just as good children generally make good parents. Selfishness, immaturity, and an undisciplined, instinctual lifestyle are early indicators of possible failure in marriage."

58   **"When I look at him I notice only how fat and bald he has got":** David L. Cohn, *Love in America* (New York: Simon & Schuster, 1943), p. 152.

59   **"For he is in the trap":** Elisabeth Abbott, translator. *The Fifteen Joys of Marriage.* New York: Bramhall House, 1959.

59   **that person doesn't seem familiar anymore:** The biological anthropologist Helen Fisher in her book *Anatomy of Love* (New York: W. W. Norton, 1992, p. 57) cites

research that indicates that romantic love wanes after one to three years.

59 **"Human beings are works in progress":** Daniel Gilbert, "The Psychology of Your Future Self," TED Talk connected to his book *Stumbling on Happiness*, March 2014.

60 **I wrote a book:** Ada Calhoun, *St. Marks Is Dead: The Many Lives of America's Hippest Street* (New York: W. W. Norton, 2015).

65 **"I've had at least three marriages":** In the 1960s, Mignon McLaughlin wrote, "A successful marriage requires falling in love many times, always with the same person" ("Accent on Living," *Atlantic Monthly*, July 1965). She also said, "Youth is not enough. And love is not enough. And, if we could achieve it, enough would not be enough" (*Atlantic Monthly*, February 1966).

72 **"a craftsman's task, a goldsmith's work":** "Address of Pope Francis to Engaged Couples Preparing for Marriage," February 14, 2014.

TOAST 4: THE TRUTH ABOUT SOUL MATES

75 **"Love is something ideal":** Siegfried Unseid, *Goethe and His Publishers*, trans. Kenneth J. Northcott (Chicago: University of Chicago Press, 1996), p. 42.

75 **In 1997, soon after Nick and I:** A version of the first part of this essay ran as a Lives

column in the *New York Times Magazine*, under the headline "Misery Games," October 21, 2012.

79 **If soul mates are real, statistically speaking:** Randall Munroe, the author of the wonderful science-questions book *What If?*, writes: "Given that you have 500,000,000 potential soul mates, you'll only find true love in one lifetime out of ten thousand"; https://what-if.xkcd.com/9/.

79 **"Ronald [as he was known] would have to tolerate":** Humphrey Carpenter, *J.R.R. Tolkien: A Biography* (Boston: Houghton Mifflin, 1987), p. 74.

79 **"Only a *very* wise man":** All the Tolkien quotes in this chapter are from one letter: "To Michael Tolkien, March 6–8, 1941." Letter number 43 in *The Letters of J.R.R. Tolkien*, ed. Humphrey Carpenter (Boston: Houghton Mifflin, 1981).

82 **Tolkien and his wife bickered:** Humphrey Carpenter, *J.R.R. Tolkien: A Biography*, p. 160.

82 **One visitor recalled:** Ibid., p. 161.

82 **On summer evenings:** Ibid., pp. 246–47.

84 **The soul mate ideal appears in:** Plato, *Symposium*, 360 B.C. Translation by Benjamin Jowett; http://classics.mit.edu /Plato/symposium.html

85 **"In order not to be miserable":** Samuel

Taylor Coleridge, *Letters, Conversations and Reflections of S. T. Coleridge* (London: Edward Moxon, 1836), pp. 88–89.

85 **"If you agree to harbor another person's soul":** Thomas Moore, *Soul Mates* (New York: Harper Perennial, 1994), p. xviii.

89 **"couples that divorce after the death of a child":** One study suggested that a couple that suffers the death of a child is eight times more likely to divorce. Other studies have said that this number is inflated but agree that it is more likely. Catherine H. Rogers et al., "Long-Term Effects of the Death of a Child on Parents' Adjustment in Midlife," National Center for Biology Information, 2008.

91 **Tolkien believed that original sin was responsible:** Carpenter, *J.R.R. Tolkien: A Biography*, p. 101.

TOAST 5: FIGHTING IN RENTAL CARS

93 **"To the end, spring winds will sow disquietude":** Robert Louis Stevenson, *Virginibus Puerisque and Other Papers* (London: C. Kegan Paul & Co., 1881), p. 26. And on p. 3 he says, "Marriage is terrifying, but so is a cold and forlorn old age."

95 ***Red Badge of Courage* audiobook:** Stephen Crane, *The Red Badge of Courage*,

unabridged, read by Anthony Heald, Blackstone Audio.

96 **"We crucify one another in marriage":** Interview of James Krueger of Mons Nubifer Sanctus by the author, August 4, 2016.

96 **"Quarrels," wrote Ovid, "are the dowry":** Ovid, *The Love Books of Ovid* (Cheshire, CT: Biblo & Tannen, 1932), p. 144.

96 **"Nothing," he said:** Claire Dederer suggests that those two lines—"What?" "Nothing?"—could constitute an entire play about marriage. Claire Dederer, *Poser* (New York: Farrar, Straus and Giroux, 2010), p. 183.

97 **"For some unknowable reason—which may have to do with the sex act":** Sparrow, letter to the author, June 7, 2016.

100 **picked up the flag and charged:** I recently exchanged e-mails with the Stephen Crane scholar Paul Sorrentino, who told me, "More than any other battle during the Civil War, this one [the Battle of Chancellorsville, on which *Red Badge* is based] revealed the tragic irony of combat. Although Robert E. Lee won the battle, it was a Pyrrhic victory. The Confederate army suffered enormous casualties and lost its brilliant General 'Stonewall' Jackson, who was accidentally wounded by his own men during the battle

and died shortly thereafter." E-mail to the author, August 31, 2016.

102 **"We reach out for help at odd points"**: Frank Bruni, "The Myth of Quality Time," *New York Times*, September 5, 2015. See also Edward S. Gleason, *Redeeming Marriage* (Cambridge, MA: Cowley, 1988), p. 143: "There is no such thing as 'quality time.' All time is of even quality, by definition, and if we invest more in some hours than in others, then we rob ourselves and our marriage. The basic unit is time, and for one to know another and to continue to live and grow and to know more of the other, there must be time invested."

TOAST 6: OTHER PEOPLE, OTHER CITIES

105 **"O happy girls, discreet in joviality!"**: "Monogamy I" in Gerald Gould, *Monogamy: A Series of Dramatic Lyrics* (London: Allen & Unwin, 1918), p. 3.

107 **"Despite the fact that the real Nala is standing right in front of her"**: Deven Patel, *Text to Tradition: The Naisadhiyacarita and Literary Community in South Asia* (New York: Columbia University Press, 2014), p. 140.

114 **against the law in twenty-one states**: Give or take a few; the law is changing. Jolie Lee, "New Hampshire Senate Votes

to Repeal Anti-Adultery Law," *USA Today*, April 17, 2014.

116 **attraction comes on like a flu:** Bits of this chapter and Toast 2 come from a *New York Times* Modern Love column I wrote called "You May Call It Cheating, but We Don't," September 14, 2012.

118 **the Kinsey scale:** "The Kinsey Scale," KinseyInstitute.org. Retrieved May 21, 2016.

119 ***Can't I even be free when I'm asleep?:*** On the you're-still-married-when-you're-asleep tip: According to Edward Gleason's book *Redeeming Marriage*, when we're married, sleeping in the same bed counts as time together (Cambridge, MA: Cowley, 1988, p. 151).

124 **"I learned that you have to pay for indulgence":** "Episode 95: Monogamy," transcript, *This American Life*, NPR, March 6, 1998.

125 **"The gate or fence did not grow there":** G. K. Chesterton, *The Collected Works of G. K. Chesterton*, vol. 3 (San Francisco: Ignatius Press, 1990), p. 157.

126 **"Yes, your friend is exactly right":** Dr. Kelly Roberts, interview by the author, March 1, 2016.

129 **"Man, I really need to give up cocaine":** Rick Shapiro made this joke often in his

weekly Sidewalk Café set, circa 2001. When I fact-checked the joke, his publicist told me I had it right but insisted I mention he's been sober for thirty years.

130 **"one tends to think of it only in connection with":** Joan Didion, "On Self-Respect," *Slouching Towards Bethlehem* (1968; repr., New York: Farrar, Straus and Giroux, 2008), p. 145. See also: "To become civilized is to establish relationships that are not merely physical, biological or instinctive; it is to establish human relationships, relationships of an essentially symbolic kind, defined by tradition and convention and rooted in respect and obligation." Herbert Fingarette, *Confucius: The Secular as Sacred* (New York: Harper Torchbooks, 1972), p. 76.

131 **"To crave and to have are as like as a thing and its shadow":** Marilynne Robinson, *Housekeeping* (New York: Macmillan, 2004), p. 152.

134 **the 80/20 rule:** *Why Did I Get Married?*, written and directed by Tyler Perry (2007).

TOAST 7: "LOVE IS STRONG AS DEATH"

137 **"No long-term marriage is made easily":** Madeleine L'Engle, *The Irrational Season* (1977; repr., San Francisco: Harper, 1983), p. 88.

139 **"Marriage is built upon grace":** Edward S. Gleason, *Redeeming Marriage* (Cambridge, MA: Cowley, 1988), p. 123.

139 **"moments of great intensity":** Both quotes appear in Virginia Woolf, *A Writer's Diary* (1953; repr., New York: Houghton Mifflin Harcourt, 2003), p. 97.

140 **"Wowsers!":** Calvin Trillin, *About Alice* (New York: Random House, 2006), p. 5.

142 **"My beloved spake":** Song of Solomon, 2:10, King James Version.

144 **"Had I known then that my wife was dead":** Excerpt from *Man's Search for Meaning*, quoted in Dana Mack and David Blankenhorn, *The Book of Marriage* (Grand Rapids, MI: William B. Eerdmans, 2001), p. 596.

148 **Some Native American ceremonies use blankets:** Cherokee.org.

148 **"Ritual can be a sacred drama":** Interview with Rabbi Lawrence A. Hoffman by the author, July 28, 2016. This is from an e-mail he sent me with an excerpt from his book *All the World: Universalism, Particularism, and the High Holy Days*.

149 **Sarah has been married to seven men:** The Book of Tobit, 7:6–14.

150 **"Love takes off the masks":** James Baldwin, *The Fire Next Time* (1963; repr., New York: Knopf, 2013), p. 95.

152 **My right knee has started to hurt:** Judith S. Wallerstein writes about similar pain in the "Marriage as a Transformative Experience" chapter of her book *The Good Marriage* (New York: Houghton Mifflin, 1995; written with Sandra Blakeslee), p. 327, leading me to believe that one way to better appreciate your marriage is to have your knees give out.

154 **"To love somebody is not just a strong feeling":** Erich Fromm, *The Art of Loving*, (1956; repr., New York: Harper Perennial, 2006), p. 52.

160 **The long-married sometimes die at the same time:** Lisa Grunwald, "The Married Couples Who Even Death Cannot Part," *Time*, May 6, 2015.

160 **A California couple:** "California Couple, Married 67 Years, Die Holding Hands," Reuters, February 26, 2015.

160 **"I felt that if Andrew died, I would die, too":** Molly Haskell, *Love and Other Infectious Diseases* (New York: William Morrow, 1990), p. 159.

160 **"There are a lot of really broken people":** Interview of Father Paul J. Hartt by the author, January 23, 2016.

162 **the years zip by:** Gretchen Rubin's brief video *The Years Are Short*, about taking her daughter to school, is one of the more

effective tearjerkers of all time. YouTube; uploaded on June 15, 2012.

162 **they'd considered divorce:** More than half of married people say they have considered divorce, and yet more than 90 percent of couples who stayed together through serious trouble were glad they hadn't divorced. See the National Divorce Decision-Making Project, *What Are They Thinking? A National Survey of Married Individuals Who Are Thinking About Divorce* (Provo, UT: Family Studies Center, Brigham Young University, 2015), and C. A. Johnson and S. M. Stanley, eds., "The Oklahoma Marriage Initiative Statewide Baseline Survey" (Stillwater, OK: Bureau for Social Research, Oklahoma State University, 2001). Of those who considered their marriage to be seriously troubled at some point (34 percent), 92 percent said they were glad they'd stayed married. In another study, 64 percent of those who said they were unhappy but stayed together reported they were happy five years later and another 25 percent reported improvement in their marriage. Linda J. Waite and Maggie Gallagher, *The Case for Marriage* (New York: Doubleday, 2000).

162 **"Many times, it simply seemed easier to stay":** Elinor Nauen, "I: Inertia," in *My*

Marriage A to Z: A Big-City Romance (El Paso, TX: Cinco Puntos Press, 2011). And interview by the author, February 4, 2016.

163 **"That it isn't about the Golden Anniversary at all":** Leah Furnas, "The Longly-Weds Know" in *To Love One Another: Poems Celebrating Marriage*, ed. Ginny Lowe Connors (West Hartford, CT: Poetworks/Grayson Books, 2002). See also the Paul Muldoon ten-year-anniversary poem "Long Finish." Paul Muldoon, *Poems, 1968–1998* (New York: Farrar, Straus and Giroux, 2001).

166 **Thomas Jefferson sat by his wife's bedside:** *Thomas Jefferson*, directed by Ken Burns (Public Broadcasting Service, 1997).

EPILOGUE: ONE TOAST I WOULD ACTUALLY GIVE

169 **"There is sure to be another flood":** William Shakespeare, *As You Like It*, Folger Shakespeare Library edition (New York: Simon & Schuster, 1997), pp. 191–92 (act 5, scene 4, lines 39–41).

174 **"The estate of marriage has universally fallen":** From Martin Luther, *The Estate of Marriage* (1522), in *Luther's Works*, vol. 45, ed. Walther I. Brandt (Minneapolis: Fortress Press, 1962).

174 **"That marriage is a failure none but the very stupid"**: Emma Goldman, *Marriage and Love* (New York: Mother Earth, 1914), p. 4.

175 **"This at last is bone of my bones"**: Genesis 2:18–24: English Standard Version. A discussion of this passage and its relevance to the Catholic wedding ceremony appears in Joseph M. Champlin, *Together for Life* (Notre Dame, IN: Ave Maria Press, 2012), p. 18.

175 **"a moment of eternity and eternal return"**: Jacob Neusner, *The Enchantments of Judaism: Rites of Transformation from Birth Through Death* (New York: Basic Books, 1987), p. 65. There's a great description of the meaning behind the Jewish marriage ceremony in chapter 4, "The Marriage Ceremony: *You* and *I* Become Adam and Eve."

176 **"The Jewish way of appreciating life at its finest"**: Interview with Rabbi Lawrence A. Hoffman by the author, July 28, 2016.

ACKNOWLEDGMENTS

181 **No. 41:** Ari Isaacman Astles, Samarth Bhaskar, and Danny DeBelius, "The Top 100 New York Times Stories of 2015, by Total Time Spent," *New York Times*, December 29, 2015.

Bibliography

"Address of Pope Francis to Engaged Couples Preparing for Marriage," February 14, 2014.

Akerlof, George A. "Men Without Children." *Economic Journal* 108, no. 447 (March 1998), pp. 287–309.

Anderson, Sherwood. *Many Marriages*. New York: B. W. Huebsch, 1923.

Angel, Katherine. *Unmastered*. New York: Farrar, Straus and Giroux, 2013.

Balzac, Honoré de. *The Physiology of Marriage*. Baltimore: Johns Hopkins University Press, 1997. Originally published in 1829.

Bane, Mary Jo. *Here to Stay: American Families in the Twentieth Century*. New York: Basic Books, 1976.

Bataille, Georges. *Erotism*. San Francisco: City Lights, 1986. Originally published in French in 1957 and in English in 1962.

Benshea, Noah, and Jordan Benshea. *A World of Ways to Say 'I Do.'* New York: McGraw-Hill, 2005.

Bergner, Daniel. *What Do Women Want?* New York: HarperCollins, 2013.

Bolick, Kate. *Spinster*. New York: Broadway Books, 2015.

Bombeck, Erma. *A Marriage Made in Heaven.* New York: HarperCollins, 1993.

Boo, Katherine. "The Marriage Cure," *New Yorker*, August 18, 2003.

Botton, Alain de. "Why You Will Marry the Wrong Person," *New York Times*, May 28, 2016.

Bright, Susie. *The Sexual State of the Union.* New York: Touchstone, 1997.

Brooks, David. "Three Views of Marriage," *New York Times*, February 23, 2016.

Burroughs, Augusten. *Lust and Wonder.* New York: St. Martin's, 2016.

Carpenter, Edward. *Love's Coming-of-Age: A Series of Papers on the Relations of the Sexes.* London: Swan Sonnenschein, 1909.

Carson, Anne. *Eros the Bittersweet.* London: Dalkey Archive, 2005.

Cather, Willa. *My Mortal Enemy.* New York: Vintage Classics, 1990. Originally published in 1926.

Champlin, Joseph M., with Peter A. Jarret. *Together for Life.* 5th ed. Notre Dame, IN: Ave Maria Press, 2012.

Chapman, Gary. *The 5 Love Languages.* Chicago: Northfield, 1995.

———. *The 4 Seasons of Marriage.* Carol Stream, IL: Tyndale, 2005.

———. *Things I Wish I'd Known Before We Got Married.* Chicago: Northfield, 2010.

Cherlin, Andrew J. "In the Season of Marriage, a Question. Why Bother?" *New York Times*, April 27, 2013.

———. *The Marriage-Go-Round*. New York: Knopf, 2009.

Chih I and T'ien Ju. *Pure Land Buddhism: Dialogues with Ancient Masters*. Translated by Thich Thien Tam. New York: Sutra Translation Committee of the United States and Canada, 1992.

Clark, Elizabeth A. *St. Augustine on Marriage and Sexuality*. Washington, DC, 1996.

Cohn, David L. *Love in America: An Informal Study of Manners and Morals in American Marriage*. New York: Simon & Schuster, 1943.

Collins, Gail. *America's Women*. New York: Perennial, 2003.

Coontz, Stephanie. *Marriage, a History*. New York: Viking, 2005.

———. *The Way We Really Are*. New York: Basic Books, 1997.

Cooper, Jilly. *How to Stay Married*. London: Bantam, 1969. Reissued in 2011.

Cott, Nancy F. *Public Vows: A History of Marriage and the Nation*. Cambridge, Massachusetts, 2000.

Cox, R. David. *Bond and Covenant*. New York: Church Publishing, 1999.

Cranmer, Thomas. *The Book of Common Prayer*.

Several versions, with approved gender-neutral marriage services and other updates, are available online at justus.anglican.org.

Daum, Meghan. *The Unspeakable*. New York: Farrar, Straus and Giroux, 2014.

Dederer, Claire. *Poser*. New York: Farrar, Straus and Giroux, 2010.

Driscoll, Mark Grace. *Real Marriage*. Nashville: Thomas Nelson, 2012. Druckerman, Pamela. *Lust in Translation*. New York: Penguin, 2007.

Easton, Dossie, and Janet W. Hardy. *The Ethical Slut*. 2nd ed. Berkeley: Celestial Arts, 2009. Originally published in 1997.

Eby, Clare Virginia. *Until Choice Do Us Part*. Chicago: University of Chicago Press, 2014.

Edin, Kathryn, and Maria Kefalas. *Promises I Can Keep*. Berkeley: University of California Press, 2005.

Eggerichs, Emerson. *Love and Respect*. Nashville: Thomas Nelson, 2004.

"*Familiaris Consortio* of Pope John Paul II," November 22, 1981.

Fingarette, Herbert. *Confucius: The Secular as Sacred*. New York: Harper Torchbooks, 1972.

Finkel, Eli J. "The All or Nothing Marriage," *New York Times*, February 14, 2014.

Fisher, Helen. *Anatomy of Love*. New York: W. W. Norton, 1992.

Ford, Arielle. *Turn Your Mate into Your Soulmate*. New York: HarperCollins, 2015.

Ford, Ford Madox. *The Good Soldier*. London: John Lane, 1915.

Franklin, Benjamin. *Reflections on Courtship and Marriage: In Two Letters to a Friend*. London: A. Thomson, 1779.

Fromm, Erich. *The Art of Loving*. New York: Harper Perennial, 2006. Originally published in 1956.

Fuller, Edmund. *The Corridor*. London: Corgi Books, 1963.

Giddens, Anthony. *The Transformation of Intimacy*. Stanford University Press, 1992.

Gilbert, Elizabeth. *Committed*. New York: Viking, 2010.

Ginzburg, Natalia. "He and I." Translated by Dick Davis, in *The Art of the Personal Essay*, edited by Phillip Lopate. New York: Anchor, 1994.

Glass, Shirley P. *Not "Just Friends."* New York: Free Press, 2003.

Gleason, Edward S. *Redeeming Marriage*. Cambridge, MA: Cowley, 1988.

Goldman, Emma. *Marriage and Love*. New York: Mother Earth, 1914.

Gottman, John M., and Nan Silver. *The Seven Principles for Making Marriage Work*. New York: Crown, 1999.

Gould, Gerald. *Monogamy: A Series of Dramatic*

Lyrics. London: Geo. Allen & Unwin, 1918.

Gould, Terry. *The Lifestyle*. Toronto: Random House of Canada, 1999.

Graff, E. J. *What Is Marriage For?* Boston: Beacon, 1999.

Grimes, Ronald L. *Deeply into the Bone: Re-Inventing Rites of Passage*. Berkeley: University of California Press, 2000.

Haag, Pamela. *Marriage Confidential*. New York: HarperCollins, 2011.

Haltzman, Scott. *The Secrets of Happily Married Men*. San Francisco: Jossey-Bass, 2007.

Hanauer, Cathi, ed. *Bitch in the House*. New York: William Morrow, 2002.

Harley, Willard F., Jr. *His Needs, Her Needs*. Ada, MI: Revell, 2011.

Harris, Lis. *Rules of Engagement: Four Couples and American Marriage Today*. New York: Simon & Schuster, 1995.

Haskell, Molly. *Love and Other Infectious Diseases*. New York: William Morrow, 1990.

Havemann, Ernest. "The Intricate Balance of a Happy Marriage." *Life*, September 29, 1961.

Hendrix, Harville. *Getting the Love You Want*. 25th anniversary ed. New York: Henry Holt, 2007.

Hippel, Theodor Gottlieb von. *On Marriage*. Translated and with an introduction by Timothy F. Sellner. Detroit: Wayne State University Press, 1994.

Hoffman, Lawrence A. *All the World: Universalism, Particularism, and the High Holy Days*. Woodstock, VT: Jewish Lights, 2014.

Hooks, Bell. "Inspired Eccentricity." In *Belonging*. London: Rout ledge, 2008.

————. *Salvation: Black People and Love*. New York: Harper Perennial, 2001.

Hymowitz, Kay, et al. "Knot Yet: The Benefits and Costs of Delayed Marriage in America." Report cosponsored by National Marriage Project, National Campaign to Prevent Teen and Unplanned Pregnancy, and Relate Institute. March 15, 2013.

James, Henry, "Is Marriage Holy?" *Atlantic Monthly*, March 1870, pp. 360–67.

Johnson, Sue. *Hold Me Tight*. New York: Little, Brown, 2008.

The Kama Sutra of Vatsyayana. Paris: Editions de la Fontaine d'Or, 1958.

Karbo, Karen. *Generation Ex: Tales from the Second Wives Club*. New York: Bloomsbury, 2001.

Keller, Timothy. *The Meaning of Marriage*. New York: Riverhead, 2013.

Key, Ellen. *Love and Marriage*. Translated from the Swedish by Arthur G. Chater. With a critical and biographical introduction by Havelock Ellis. New York: G. P. Putnam's Sons, 1911.

Kipnis, Laura. *Against Love*. New York: Pantheon, 2003.

Kramer, Peter. *Should You Leave?* New York: Penguin, 1997.

Kraus, Chris. *I Love Dick*. Los Angeles: Semiotext(e)/Native Agents, 1997.

Laing, Olivia. *The Lonely City*. New York: Picador, 2016.

Lamm, Maurice. *The Jewish Way in Love and Marriage*. Middle Village, NY: Jonathan David Publishers, 1991.

Lamott, Anne. *Small Victories*. New York: Riverhead, 2014.

Lawson, Annette. Adultery: *An Analysis of Love and Betrayal*. New York: Basic Books, 1988.

L'Engle, Madeleine. *The Irrational Season*. New York: Farrar, Straus and Giroux, 1977.

——. *Two-Part Invention: The Story of a Marriage*. New York: Farrar, Straus and Giroux, 1988.

Lewis, C. S. *The Four Loves*. New York: Harcourt, 1988. Originally published in 1960.

Levy, John, and Ruth Monroe, *The Happy Family*. New York: Knopf, 1945.

Lobsenz, Norman M., and Clark W. Blackburn. *How to Stay Married*. New York: Cowles, 1968.

Loh, Sandra Tsing. "Let's Call the Whole Thing Off." *Atlantic*, July–August 2009.

————. *The Madwoman in the Volvo*. New York: W. W. Norton, 2014.

Lopate, Phillip. *Two Marriages*. New York: Other Press, 2008.

Macfarlane, Julie. *Understanding Trends in American Marriage: Muslim Divorce and Marriage.* Washington, DC: Institute for Social Policy and Understanding, 2016.

Mace, David and Vera Mace. Marriage: East and West. Garden City, NY: Dolphin, 1960.

Mack, Dana, and David Blankenhorn. *The Book of Marriage: The Wisest Answers to the Toughest Questions.* Grand Rapids, MI: William B. Eerdmans, 2001.

Mackey, Richard A., and Bernard A. O'Brien. *Lasting Marriages: Men and Women Growing Together*. Westport, CT: Praeger, 1995.

Madsen, Pamela. *Shameless*. New York: Rodale, 2011.

Manguso, Sarah. *Ongoingness*. New York: Graywolf, 2015.

————. *The Two Kinds of Decay: A Memoir*. New York: Farrar, Straus and Giroux, 2008.

Markman, Howard J., and Scott M. Stanley. *Fighting for Your Marriage*. San Francisco: Jossey-Bass, 1994.

"Marriage: A Discussion Guide for Families and Communities," Institute for Social Policy and Understanding, 2012.

Marriage, Religion, and Modern Life. CBSNews. com, December 13, 2015.

Mason, Mike. *The Mystery of Marriage*. Portland, OR: Multnomah, 1985.

McCafferty, Jane. *First You Try Everything*. New York: Harper, 2012.

Miller, David. *The Secret of the Jew: His Life—His Family*. Vol. 1. New York: Committee of Rabbi David Miller Foundation, 1930.

Miller, Michael Vincent. *Intimate Terrorism: The Deterioration of Erotic Life*. New York: W. W. Norton, 1995.

Millet, Catherine. *Jealousy: The Other Life of Catherine M.* New York: Grove, 2008.

Millet, Lydia. *Sweet Lamb of Heaven*. New York: W. W. Norton, 2016.

Mitchell, Stephen A. *Can Love Last?* New York: W. W. Norton, 2002.

Moore, Thomas. *Soul Mates*. New York: Harper Perennial, 1994.

Munro, Alice. *Hateship, Friendship, Loveship, Courtship, Marriage*. New York: Vintage, 2001.

Munson, Laura. *This Is Not the Story You Think It Is . . .* New York: Berkley, 2010.

Nauen, Elinor. *My Marriage A to Z: A Big-City Romance*. El Paso, TX: Cinco Puntos, 2011.

Nelson, Maggie. *The Argonauts*. New York: Graywolf, 2015.

————. *The Art of Cruelty*. New York: W. W. Norton, 2011.

Neusner, Jacob. *The Enchantments of Judaism: Rites of Transformation from Birth Through Death*. New York: Basic Books, 1987.

Offill, Jenny. *Dept. of Speculation*. New York: Vintage, 2014.

"*Parabhava Sutta*: Downfall." In *Collected Wheel Publications*, vols. 1–15. Kandy, Sri Lanka: Buddhist Publication Society, 2008. (On p. 348: "Not to be contented with one's own wife, and to be seen with harlots and the wives of others—this is a cause of one's downfall.")

Parker-Pope, Tara. *For Better: The Science of a Good Marriage*. New York: Dutton, 2010.

————. "The Happy Marriage Is the 'Me' Marriage." *New York Times*, December 31, 2010.

Parrott, Les, and Leslie Parrott. *Saving Your Marriage Before It Starts*. Grand Rapids, MI: Zondervan, 1995.

Paul, Pamela. *The Starter Marriage and the Future of Matrimony*. New York: Villard, 2002.

Perel, Esther. *Mating in Captivity*. New York: Harper, 2006.

Plump, Wendy. *Vow: A Memoir of Marriage (and Other Affairs)*. New York: Bloomsbury, 2013.

Pollitt, Katha. *Learning to Drive*. New York: Random House, 2007.

Pontano, Giovani Giovano. *On Married Love and Eridanus*. Translated by Luke Roman. Cambridge, MA: Harvard University Press, 2014.

Ponteri, Jay. *Wedlocked*. Portland, OR: Hawthorne, 2013.

Renou, Louis, ed. *Hinduism*. New York: George Braziller, 1962.

Roiphe, Anne. *Married: A Fine Predicament*. New York: Basic Books, 2002.

Rosen, Ruth. *The World Split Open*. New York: Penguin, 2000.

Rothbart, Davy. *My Heart Is an Idiot*. New York: Farrar, Straus and Giroux, 2012.

Rubin, Lillian B. *Just Friends*. New York: Harper & Row, 1985.

Ruiz, Don Miguel. *The Mastery of Love*. San Rafael, CA: Amber-Allen, 1999.

Rush, Norman. *Mortals*. New York: Vintage, 2003.

Ryan, Christopher, and Cacilda Jetha. *Sex at Dawn*. New York: Harper, 2010.

Ryerson, James. "Love in the Time of Monogamy," *New York Times*, April 5, 2016.

Savage, Dan. *The Commitment*. New York: Dutton, 2005.

Scharfstein, Ben-Ami. *Ineffability*. Albany: State University of New York Press, 1993.

Schlessinger, Laura. *The Proper Care and Feeding of Husbands*. New York: Harper Perennial, 2006.

Schnarch, David. *The Passionate Marriage*. New York: W. W. Norton, 1997.

Schwartz, Lynne Sharon. *Rough Strife*. New York: Harper & Row, 1980.

Shapiro, Dana Adam. *You Can Be Right (or You Can Be Married)*. New York: Scribner, 2012.

Shaw, George Bernard. *Getting Married*. Studio City, CA: Players Press, 1995. Originally published in 1908.

Stephens, Autumn, ed. *The Secret Lives of Lawfully Wedded Wives*. Maui: Inner Ocean, 2006.

Stevenson, Robert Louis. *Virginibus Puerisque and Other Papers*. London: C. Kegan Paul & Co., 1881.

Stopes, Marie Carmichael. *Married Love: A New Contribution to the Solution of Sex Differences*. New York: G. P. Putnam's Sons, 1931.

Strayed, Cheryl. *Tiny Beautiful Things*. New York: Vintage, 2012.

Strossen, Nadine. *Defending Pornography*. New York: New York University Press, 2000. Originally published in 1995.

Talese, Gay. *Thy Neighbor's Wife*. New York: Harper Perennial, 2009. Originally published in 1980.

Taylor, John. *Falling: The Story of One Marriage*. New York: Random House, 1999.

Texier, Catherine. *Breakup: The End of a Love Story*. New York: Doubleday, 1998.

Thorold, A. W. *On Marriage*. New York: H. M. Caldwell, 2010.

Townsend, John. *Boundaries in Marriage*. Grand Rapids, MI: Zondervan, 2002.

Traister, Rebecca. *All the Single Ladies*. New York: Simon & Schuster, 2016.

Trillin, Calvin. *About Alice*. New York: Random House, 2006.

Turnbull, Colin M. *The Human Cycle*. New York: Simon & Schuster, 1983.

Tyler, Anne. *Breathing Lessons*. New York: Ballantine, 1988.

Updike, John. *Too Far to Go*. New York: Fawcett, 1982. Originally published in 1979.

Utley, Ebony A. "When Better Becomes Worse: Black Wives Describe Their Experiences with Infidelity." *Black Women, Gender, and Families* 5, no. 1 (Spring 2011), pp. 66–89.

Van de Velde, Th. H. *Ideal Marriage: Its Physiology and Technique*. Translated by Stella Browne. New York: Random House, 1930.

Viorst, Judith. *Grown-up Marriage*. New York: Free Press, 2003.

Waldman, Ayelet. *Bad Mother*. New York: Doubleday, 2009.

———. "Truly, Madly, Guiltily." *New York Times*, March 27, 2005.

Wallerstein, Judith S., and Sandra Blakeslee. *The Good Marriage*. New York: Houghton Mifflin, 1995.

Weil, Elizabeth. *No Cheating, No Dying*. New York: Scribner, 2012.

Weisser, Susan Ostrov. *Women and Romance: A Reader*. New York: New York University Press, 2001.

Yalom, Marilyn. *A History of the Wife*. New York: HarperCollins, 2001.

Yates, Richard. *Revolutionary Road*. New York: Vintage, 1961.

Yuknavitch, Lidia. *The Chronology of Water*. Portland, OR: Hawthorne, 2010.

Books are produced
in the United States
using U.S.-based
materials

Books are printed
using a revolutionary
new process called
THINKtech™ that
lowers energy usage
by 70% and increases
overall quality

Books are durable
and flexible because
of smythe-sewing

Paper is sourced
using environmentally
responsible foresting
methods and the
paper is acid-free

Center Point Large Print
600 Brooks Road / PO Box 1
Thorndike, ME 04986-0001 USA

(207) 568-3717

US & Canada:
1 800 929-9108
www.centerpointlargeprint.com